FINAL APPROACH

Early on I decided if I were to tell this story, the book would have a greater good for the lives of others.

So here is the deal! Although this book is about my life, it is really about helping those that may be headed down the dark path I chose early on.

Proceeds from the sale of the book will go to **Our Y, Sarasota's Family Gym**, for their continued support of me and my brother Gregory. My profits will also contribute to numerous other groups that help troubled souls dealing with suicide, substance abuse, child abuse, mental and physical abuse.

With your help purchasing this book, we can be a positive force for goodness long after my time on Earth has expired. And if you decide not to buy the book, please consider donating to Our Y yourself. Seriously my friend, this statement and book are no bullshit!

Peace and God bless you and yours,
Jerome Lill
☮ Out!!

FINAL APPROACH
In the Battle of Angels
It's a God Thing

**The Raw and Candid Story of a
Marijuana Smuggler and Alcoholic
Who Found Redemption**

by

JEROME LILL

QUARRIER PRESS
Charleston, West Virginia

Quarrier Press
Charleston, WV

Printed in the United States of America.

Editorial Production by Andrea Doherty
Book Design and production by Norman C. Lyle

10 9 8 7 6 5 4 3 2 1

ISBN 13: 978-1-942294-27-6
ISBN 10: 1-942294-27-1

Distributed by:

West Virginia Book Company
1125 Central Ave.
Charleston, WV 25302
www.wvbookco.com

Man, you did one huge thing; (with God's help, because it's a God thing and easier to say than do) — you forgave your parents, your grandparents...and through your book, apologized to those you hurt or let down...you can use your blessings to bless others. That's where I believe we find our purpose in life.

—Tim DiPiero
Former Assistant U.S. Attorney 1977-1983
who put me in the slammer for the 1979 pot plane crash
(which, in the end, turned out to be a blessing)
Thanks Tim!

I am compelled to tell you the immense pleasure I had in reading your remarkable book. Not only are the events of your life extraordinary, but the telling of the story is uniquely authentic and sincere...You should be commended on your outstanding work...a story very well told.

—Ron Samarian, M.D.
Diplomate, American Board of Psychiatry and Neurology

It had a little of everything...funny, sad, exciting, ironic, iconic, quite an adventure.

—Brian Munce
Detroiter

Returning to Detroit from Sarasota, where I was visiting my brother Gregory, I met a couple who were also returning to Michigan on the same flight. I noticed they were both reading, and I offered them a copy of this book. I asked them to read the book, and if they would like to respond, to email me their opinion, whether positive or negative. Within two days, I received the following email:

Dear Jerome (Jerry):

I just wanted to let you know I've read your book the last two days and thoroughly enjoyed the read! I can see now why you wanted to write your story!!

I found that the book flowed easily, and it was very easy reading; kept my attention. I truly didn't want to put it down until I read it entirely. Yes, there were parts that were tough to read. For example, all the people and animals you lost over the years. That is truly SAD!!! And how alcoholism and drug addiction risked your life numerous times. You ARE so lucky to be alive!! It really helped to read that you know that now!!

You've had so many incredible experiences in your life as well, which is clearly what molded you into who you are presently.

I'm a mother of four grown adults. Been married for 35 years, taught special ed for 32 years and now have been a clinical psychologist for the past 4-1/2 years. So I guess you could say, I read your book from many angles. I also thought of the countless people I have counseled with addiction issues.

Yet, what intrigued me the most was your journey that lead you to your faith! That is definitely the icing on the top of your story. I do feel you can and will help many people with the same struggles; see that they can quit that life style (with love and support) - AND also find hope and a future through faith/God!

Each person has their own struggles that can lead them to building a strong relationship with God (higher power, etc). Yet the main focus is He is the answer! Faith is the answer to each of our tough challenges. You make that loud and clear in your book, which I'm sure you fully intended! So for that reason, that was the favorite part of your book for me. The message is clear: If you can find God through all the 'shit' you went through....anyone can!!!

So. After my husband gets done reading and enjoying your book - (because I know he will also love it) - then we will pass it on to each of our kids to begin with. I can also recommend it to my clients as well. I do think a great place for you to target your book is rehabs/mental health clinics across the globe.....but you probably already know that.

In closing, thanks so much for noticing we love to read on the plane and sharing your passion with us! We feel blessed to have met you. Btw, we too have our own very strong faith stories as well, so we could really relate to how great God is!!!

May you continue to be blessed on your journey! Stay safe. Stay healthy and God bless!!!

Pam McMillan
(From the flight back from Sarasota on Nov 12, 2020!)

Ps: the hamburgers were delicious!!!!

Here's the CARES Act; Gregory Lill, my
brother, was stricken with the COVID-19
virus early on. Gregory, however, was
praying for everyone else who had it.
Now that is how you spell "HERO!"
Quit complaining! Someone else
always has it worse than you or me!

I surely did not plan to finish my book during the *"pandammit,"* my name for the COVID-19 pandemic. This is now a Battle of Angels! If you're bad, get good! If you're good, get better! The hatred and evil is far more dangerous than any virus! Loss of old friendships and anger can destroy more than COVID ever could. The stories I tell you are the stories of lifestyles of the dumb and dangerous. And that's exactly how we as humans are now acting. Please pay attention and pray for others—not just for yourself.

*I would like to thank the following people
for helping to make this book possible:*

First, more than anyone else, I want to thank God for showing me the path to redemption and sobriety. And I want to thank all of my "fallen angels," without whom I might not be here today.

Special thanks go to my brother Greg, for sharing his strength with me. I couldn't have done this without you Greg.

Thanks to Norm Lyle for helping me with the design and production of this book, and the valuable counsel he has given me throughout this process, and for putting up with me when I was a fucking drunk.

And thanks to Andrea Doherty, my executive editor; Ben Rose for helping me with the original audio for the book, and for helping me get started.

My sister Joanne for always being there.

My vascular surgeon, Steven Silver for saving my limbs and my life.

Glen Heidrich, for letting me stay at his house while I wrapped up this book.

And extra-special thanks to my good friend and mentor, Lawrence Otto Heidrich. RIP Larry. Thanks.

Table of Contents

What Kind of Man Am I?

My name is Jerome Lill, and I have one bizarre story. This is a tale about smuggling, alcoholism, substance abuse, and general recklessness that only led to even more smuggling, alcoholism, substance abuse and recklessness. It's the true story of my life and, like many others' lives, full of ups and downs. I've seen a lot of shit in my day, enough to make you think, *"Is this guy for real?"*

Well, yeah, this guy's *all too real.*

The real story I want to share with you is about how I turned a whole lot of self abuse into self love. When you think about it, that's all alcoholism and substance abuse is—self abuse. Man, you have to learn to love yourself for exactly who you are before you're ever going to love anyone else. It took too many lost lives for me to realize that. Too many friends and family members gone too soon.

When I was young I got caught up in it real bad. I was as bad as they come. It wasn't me and, deep down, I knew I was selling myself short. But I wasn't really looking deep into my soul at the time. I was into instant gratification, the risk, the excitement, the high. And really not caring who I hurt or stepped on.

The excitement and risk came to a crash on June 6, 1979 in Charleston, West Virginia, in Kanawha County. I crashed a DC-6 with three other guys, and 26,000 pounds of Colombian marijuana smuggled on board the aircraft. It was this very moment that reignited my faith in God. I survived a near-fatal crash and, even then, finding my way back to sobriety took decades. I fought my way out of a dead end. I battled alongside my friends, alongside the fallen angels. The difference was, I found a way out.

This collection of stories will describe my long journey to salvation. I went down a bad path, but the accident, alone, was the tipping point, and I want to share it with you.

I am certain for those of you who believe in God, this will power an even greater faith. If you don't find that faith, you will. I guarantee it.

Despite my rekindled faith, it has taken me years to get both my mind and body in the right place to tell my story and the stories of the angels who passed too soon. We'll get there in good time, but right now, I want to explain why this is the right time. What took me so long? Hell, I don't know.

No, I do know. Alcohol—of course.

I've started this book a hundred times but the problem was that I was never sober. Have you ever told a story while you were drunk? Well, probably. Drunks tell stories. I've told countless drunk tales but none very good. No one can tell a good story while they're drunk. When you're drunk, you forget details, you exaggerate details, you get the timing all wrong…it's just a mess. There's no credibility to it. No one believes it could be true.

So I had to get sober first. I needed to end the spiral I was spinning down before it was too late. I was determined to save myself so I could save others.

This is my mission. This is my story.

It doesn't have to be your story.

I'm proud to say that this is the real me today, and whoever I've wronged and fucked over, *I apologize* and I hope and pray for your forgiveness. I can't take back what I did, and if I believe you fucked me over the same way, I forgive you.

See, without forgiveness, we all rot from the inside. At some point, we've all been an asshole because we believed it wasn't about anyone else. It was all about ourselves and how we can get what we want in any way possible, no matter who we fuck over to get there. I guess what I'm saying is that we're all assholes at one time or another. If you can't admit that, then you're probably still an asshole. I was one of the biggest assholes, so I know it's true. Once I finally stopped filling my body and mind with poison, my "asshole-ism" went right into remission, and it's been in remission for a long time.

I feel great about who I am today. I spread positivity, I spread love. All of that was stolen from me because of the poisons of substance abuse, the thrill of a wild ride. These people from the straight and narrow—they fell hard. I did, too. Lucky for me, I woke up after a lot of living and almost dying.

There is hope for all human beings, even in these turbulent times. The beauty is truly discovered when you dig your way out of the shit – you see exactly how beautiful life can be.

We're in a constant battle and we all have a duty to see ourselves through by spreading love, spreading joy, spreading faith in each other. This is why I call the book *In The Battle of Angels.* Every one of us are angels in battle. We're fighting to keep our shit together. So pay close attention to what I have to say.

This book is dedicated to all the people that I've known who have died because of drugs and alcohol abuse, and depression, suicide–all kinds of shit.

I'd like to dedicate it to my father, who was a major alcoholic and used to beat the shit out of me.

I want to dedicate it to my grandparents who introduced me to alcohol when I was six years old; and my uncle Fernie; Brian Schaffer, who was my best friend and died in a car accident at 18 where alcohol was a factor.

Larry Bergland, failed liver; George Woods, suicide; Jimmy Heidrich blew his brains out; Dennis Housdorf drank himself to death; Mike Marsh drank himself to death; Ernest Mannes, one of my boat captains, drank himself to death; Jeff Special, heroin addict; Mike Special and Mishelle Special, both alcoholics; Bobby Zingg blew his brains out; Greg Hickey, liver; Pat Hickey, liver; Jim Miekle, suicide;

Hal O'Connor, car accident, alcohol; Skip Bond, car accident, alcohol; Elaine Heick, heroin; Jerry Wojack, liver.

Dick Sloss, cocaine-induced stroke; George Marcus, liver; Mary Gunsmar, liver; Pear Hare, shot himself in the head with a double-barreled shotgun; John Cole, missing in action; Denny Potts just blew his brains out; George, drank himself to death; Randy, drank himself to death, heroin; Gary Rodgers, liver; Sue, my cousin, alcohol; Janet, my cousin, alcohol; Mike Allen blew his brains out; Crissy shot himself; Joann, alcohol, liver; Dave Brady, alcohol, liver; Bob Sopellic, car accident, alcohol; Sharon, cocaine overdose; Glenn, heroin.

Fred "Sonic" Smith of the MC5, alcohol; Jimmy Chadwick shot himself; Danny Switzer drank himself to death; Chuck Manko, murder, heroin dealer; Skip Julius, suicide; Mike Murphy, suicide; Jimmy Johnson, alcohol; Greg Allman, alcohol; Robbie Robinson, murdered, alcohol, cocaine; Dee, a .357 blew his brains out; Janine, she's dying right now; Terry Spearie, cocaine/alcohol; Eric Ward, alcohol; Cindi, alcohol; and Dennis Regal, drowned, alcohol.

All these people died because of alcohol or drugs or depression. In a way, they were all forms of suicide. You know, when you stop and boil it down, it all has to do with self-abuse. It should have never happened to them. Hell, it should never happen to anyone. Period. They were my friends, they were good people, they all touched my life, and they were all gone too soon. They just got caught up in the shit, you know?

You need to hear this story so you don't get caught up in the shit, too. It's easy to jump on a path that, at first, seems exciting and sexy. The drinks, fun, smoking, money, drugs, women—it all seems worth the risk. But it's not. It's not worth the risk because once your plane is going down, you don't have a lot of time to find a parachute.

CHAPTER ONE

Keep Pushin' On

I was born in Detroit, Michigan at Detroit Women's Hospital, which probably has something to do with my addiction to women. Once upon a time, I was what you might call a womanizer, but let's save that for later. Of course, I still love women today—not gonna apologize for that!

My father's mother, Grandma Lill, introduced me to alcohol when I was, like, six years old. I had a toothache, so Grandma Lill loaded me up with alcohol before we went downtown to see the dentist.

I distinctly remember the moment that alcohol hit my bloodstream because I felt good. Now, dig this, six years old and I've got this little old lady, 5'2", nursing me on alcohol. That's fucked up, but I liked it. I liked how I could feel the warmth spreading through my chest, then into my belly. That planted the seed of alcoholism for me. I imagine that's why my father was fucked up from an early age, too. Because if Grandma was giving me alcohol at six years old, I'm pretty sure my dad got his first taste just as early as I did.

Soon after all that shit, we moved to Beverly Hills, Michigan from Detroit. My dad was rising up the ranks where he worked at Detroit National Bank and Trust, which was merging with Manufacturer's National Bank at the time. After that deal went down, my dad decided he was a rich big shot and bought a house in Beverly Hills – a step up in the world. According to my racist father, his deal was to "get away from the niggers." I grew up listening to all that racist shit, and I didn't agree with it at all. It was messed up. He didn't see people for who they were inside, he didn't see them for the goodness they had inside.

Hard to see that stuff through a bottle.

Anyhow, my father liked to beat kids up. Not kids. Me, actually.

It didn't really matter what I did because, after he had a few cocktails, he just liked to punch me. Of course I didn't appreciate that, but what the fuck was I supposed to do? I was just a little kid whose only defense was to get away from him as quickly as I could. My older brother Greg used to tell me "Run Jerry, RUN!" It was just like that scene in Forrest Gump. *Run Forrest Run!*

My mother turned a blind eye towards that shit. She pretended it didn't happen because as long as my father was making money for her to spend, he could do whatever the fuck he wanted. You could say my mother was kind of whacked out too. She loved the money like my father loved drinking and taking it all out on me.

She was blind to all of it, to be honest with you.

Some of this shit still hurts to think about today, believe me. The funny thing is, after all of the abuse and neglect, I don't hate my mother. Hell, I don't even hate my father. I realize now they were dysfunctional, fucked up people who got caught up in a cycle of dysfunction, just like I did.

Anyway, I just wanted to stay out of the house whenever possible, which led me to all kinds of trouble when we were living in Beverly Hills. I couldn't seem to do anything right in my father's eyes so I just had as much fun as I could, which means I was trouble. Real trouble. My father was always ready to knock the shit out of me. Now, I'm not talking about spankings. I'm talking about getting the *fucking shit beat out of you.*

Anyway, time went on and nothing changed until 1961 when I got really sick with encephalitis. My mother used to go out a lot while my dad went to the bank. One day I came down with the mumps, and my parents just told me to stay inside while they were gone. You can imagine how well behaved I was by this point. Well, the mumps can turn into encephalitis, but I didn't know that shit. So I just continued to do what I wanted, which was going out and playing while they were gone. I mean, I was six years old. Of course I was going to do whatever I wanted with no parents at home. Before they came home, I'd come inside and get back in bed.

After some time with the mumps, I came down with encephalitis, or brain fever. It's an inflammation in the brain and can be deadly. My mother made me some hot strawberry Quik since I was sick and she was trying to be "motherly".

You remember strawberry Quik? It came in a plastic container and you mixed the pink powder with milk – kids loved it. After I drank a cup of that, I threw it up all over my bed. Most mothers would say *it's ok, let's get you cleaned up*, or *Oh, honey, don't worry, I know you didn't do it on purpose*. My mother? My mother smacked me and then yelled at me because she had to change the sheets. What the fuck? I will never forget that shit.

So when I had encephalitis, I couldn't talk. I could hear everybody in the room—muffled—but I could make out what they were saying. I just lost control of my motor functions. I couldn't talk, I couldn't hold myself up, I couldn't walk. It's a very strange feeling. My parents used to have to take me and physically sit me up on the toilet. My father wasn't watching me closely enough and I fell off the toilet. Cracked my head open, and they had to take me to Beaumont Hospital in Royal Oak to get stitches. I'm sure it's no surprise that I got yelled at for falling off the fucking toilet even when I couldn't control myself. You bet I got smacked for that.

Encephalitis is serious shit and my fever spiked real high but I eventually recovered. Naturally, I was pissed at my parents about my treatment that time, too. I was fucking angry, and I think you would be, too. I was just a kid, but I was mad.

My dad continued his fucking drinking, even on his way to work. He'd take the train from Birmingham to downtown Detroit because, well, he really liked to drink on the train. My mother would load the car up with me and my siblings, and we all drove him to the station. At the end of the day, we picked him up and as soon as we got home, my father had a few more drinks. It didn't take long for him to think of a reason to kick my ass. This went on all the fucking time. I was the only one that got it. He didn't beat up my brother Gregory who had cerebral palsy, epilepsy, and was mentally disabled. He didn't beat my older brother Michael. My little sister Joanne was too small so he didn't beat her. He also never beat my mother. I was his fucking punching bag, to be honest with you. Like all alcoholics, my father kept saying he was going to quit drinking, but he never did.

In 1962, we moved into the Greenwich Green neighborhood, a new subdivision off 14 Mile Road in Beverly Hills, just south of Birmingham.

My father bought a big William Pulte home, across from the Lincoln Hills Golf Club. He had it built from the ground up and paid, like, $35,000. That was a lot of money in 1962. It seemed like we had a lot of money back then because my father was buying new cars and giving my mother spending money. There was no way she was going to leave because she had money. Money was "talking big" and to live in the suburbs and have new cars, that was big fucking talk. In my mother's eyes, if my dad drank, so what? She was getting her money so what did it fucking matter?

One day in 1968, he came home from work and he looked really bad. Extremely bad. I wouldn't say alcoholics look particularly healthy but he managed to compose himself for others. This day, though, he was pretty looped when he walked through the door. His skin was yellow, he was sweating, and just didn't look right. My mom told him to just go to bed and rest. She thought he'd be better in the morning.

So up to bed he went.

At some point in the middle of the night, my mother woke up and sensed something wasn't right. She felt a wet, tar-like substance on the bed. Turns out, my dad was bleeding out of his ass.

He blew a fuse, I guess we could say.

My mother reached for the phone and called his doctor. He told her to get him to the hospital right away or he'd be a dead man in the morning. I remember my father coming down the stairs and he had his hat just hanging halfway on his head.

I don't know why I remember that one detail so clearly. It's like the hat was balancing precariously on his head. One sudden movement and it would fall off. Even at 14 years old, I realized I felt like that hat. Always trying to find a balance of being a kid and being a punching bag. If I made any sudden movements, he'd start beating on me again.

As he ambled toward the door, I could tell he was fucked up. When my mother came back from the hospital, she said he was very ill and had to have an operation, but first they had to dry him out because he was getting *delirium tremens*, what we call the DTs. He was in the Intensive Care Unit at Beaumont.

My dad didn't come home for a while because the operation they had to do was pretty serious, and the recovery took some time in the hospital. The operation was only performed a handful of times, was only occasionally successful, but my father decided to go ahead and get it since it could greatly improve his condition.

The operation was successful and after he recovered in the hospital, they sent him home. A couple weeks later, he fucking croaked from complications.

To be honest, I really wasn't that upset when my dad died. It's complicated. He was my father and I loved him, but I sure wasn't going to miss getting smacked around. This guy used to punch me so hard I would throw up, puke, just nasty shit to do to a kid. *Adios, Dad.* Maybe that sounds a little cruel or cold hearted, but the man beat me!

I don't know why I never told anyone. I often went to school bruised, but since I played sports I could use that as the reason for having bruises. I was like the typical battered wife who always claimed she fell down the stairs, or is just clumsy. I "fell down" playing football or baseball a lot.

My father actually went to many of my baseball games. Most kids would be thrilled if their dad went to watch a ball game, but I knew he had other motives. His seat was generally empty for eight of the nine innings. His goal was to get a drink without my mom knowing about it.

On the way home, we stopped at the Royal Lounge on Woodward Avenue in Royal Oak. They had these huge hamburgers and my dad would bribe me with some of his beer and $5. He was trying to keep me quiet and, maybe in his own way, pay me off for beating on me.

Little did he know my mom also bribed me with $5. She gave me a five spot if I told her whether or not my dad stopped for a drink. I guess you could say I was introduced to the power of bribery early on. I didn't really care because I had a thing against both of them. It's not natural to feel that way toward your parents but what can I say?

They didn't exactly treat *me* with much tenderness. After my dad kicked my ass he would always sit me down and tell me he hits me because he loves me. I never understood that. Love does not translate to abuse and I know that now but, as a kid, I couldn't make sense of it. After my old man kicked the bucket, I really felt like the two sides of a coin. I didn't really care that he was gone, but I also missed him in a weird way.

Well, I guess you could say I missed the idea—the dream— of having a dad who would finally realize the pain he caused his family by drinking and he'd get cleaned up because he truly loved us. With him gone, that could never happen. It was that dream that I missed.

After my dad passed away, I went completely nuts. My mother had no control over me at all and I started running with a lot of other people who were just getting into doing drugs and selling pot. Actually, it was my brother, Michael, who sold me pot for the first time. I hooked up with a good buddy of mine, Brian Schaffer, and I quickly changed roles and sold pot to my brother. Incidentally, Brian's father had also just died from alcoholism and was a lawyer for General Motors.

Brian's mother had recently remarried a guy named Otto Milbrand, who owned Milbrand Maintenance. Coincidentally, Brian's stepfather's name was Otto, just like my dad. We had a lot in common, Brian and I. We became partners and decided to move our drug business into the high schools.

We started selling pot and LSD. We were soon making some serious money. I didn't care to be at home much because my family fell apart after my dad died.

Me? I just went on. I was a loose cannon. My mother couldn't control me in any way, which didn't bother me one bit. I mean, Schaffer and I just became the local marijuana and pill dealers. Between Groves High School, Seaholm High School and Shain Park in Birmingham, we were making a lot of money and had a lot of girlfriends.

Schaffer's father had left him a lot of money after he died so he was in a position to finance our business. We hooked up with another buddy of ours, Larry Bergland, and our partnership turned into a trio. Sort of a "kid's cartel." We controlled the drug sales at Groves and Seaholm. Imagine that. Two kids just makin' good money at the time.

Anyway, Brian and I weren't just selling the drugs, we were doing them and getting deeper and deeper. I met a guy named Dick Sloss.

Dickie was the manager for a popular local band called the Wilson Mower Pursuit. He was getting into the rock and roll business and was developing some connections. He was buddies with Ed "Punch" Andrews, Bob Seger's manager. For $50 a night, Dickie hired me as a roadie. With fifty bucks, I could get beer, meet girls and sell some dope. Who could want more than that?

I started working with Dickie more and I got to work for the MC5. I worked for Iggy Pop and The Stooges — at that time it was the Psychedelic Stooges, actually — Ted Nugent and the Amboy Dukes, and I carried equipment a couple times for Alice Cooper. So I was working with all these bands. We used to go out to a farm in Walled Lake where Bob "Catfish" Hodge and the band Catfish lived and rehearsed, and ran around with them too. I was running around with all these older guys, because I was still young. You're talking about a 15-year-old kid doing this.

More drugs, more partying, time after time. Me and Schaffer were, like, moving up in the scene. Eventually, Schaffer met a guy named Matthew Lochriccio, a drug dealer from the other side of Detroit. He owned a pizzeria, and Schaffer and I were getting drugs cheap from him.

Another guy named Woody Keane and his old lady, Meg, were smuggling hash from Amsterdam in puzzles. So we would invest in that and they'd send back top of the line Pakistani hash and red Lebanese hash. Blond hash and occasionally *kif*. They'd put it in puzzles and send it back to themselves at the post office.

Now, we're buying kilos at the time for $900 a pop. Sixteen ounces to a pound. A kilo—double that—and we'd get $100 an ounce. Pretty good money, especially when you're in high school. We made a ton and spent a lot of it on clothes. We bought leather pants, leather jackets. We had motorcycles — Honda 305 Scramblers — at the time. Actually, we used to go out to Stony Creek Metropark and go scrambling. Basically, we were just screwing girls, spending money, and partying.

Schaffer got a 1968 Volkswagen van — a camper. We decided to start taking trips every year because we were making so much money. We saved up our money through the high school year, and used our parents' houses as stash houses for our money and dope. We really didn't go to school too much because we were too busy running around Birmingham, hustling drugs.

Ultimately, Brian noticed that our third partner, Larry, wasn't paying his part of what was supposed to be coming in. So Brian wanted to kick him out of the group. I kind of felt sorry for Larry. I told Schaffer we should just keep him anyway. But Brian insisted on getting rid of Larry, so Larry was out. Schaffer and I just went out to California and Colorado every summer.

On one particular trip out west we picked up some hitchhikers as we were heading home from California in the summer of '69, which was a pretty cool time. We were going to drop them in Chicago and they told us about a festival that was going to happen in New York.

Woodstock.

So we stopped in Chicago so these hitchhikers could pick up some things. Then we stopped in Detroit so Schaffer and I could pick up more money and drugs, because naturally we were going to sell drugs at Woodstock, right? Why not?

So we took these two hitchhikers, one guy called himself Jesus, and I don't remember what the other guy's name was. Then there was this chick named Crazy Connie. So we took Connie, Jesus and his sidekick, and we went to Woodstock.

Needless to say, I made a lot of money at Woodstock. I watched Jimi Hendrix play the Star Spangled Banner at 9:00 in the morning. Saw tons of bands. We saw The Who and Janis Joplin with her Kozmic Blues Band. Crosby, Stills & Nash, Ten Years After, Joe Cocker.

One night, tripping, I stepped out of our VW and the audience had lit thousands of candles. It seemed to me I was looking at a field of angels—I really thought that! I even yelled for Schaffer to come out and look. Too much acid *ya think?* I'll never forget those few days at Woodstock.

As I said, God's watching your ass all the time. Long time back, when I was in high school, my old partner, Brian Schaffer and I had gone out to Dick Sloss' house; they were having a party out there.

That was in the period when we were all taking plenty of Tuinols, and Brian was smoking what we used to call "Angeldust." Marijuana, chemically enhanced with PCP. Very strong shit.

Brian had tried to pick up a cute girl, but she was having none of it. She slapped him for some reason, and Brian went ballistic. I watched him run outside and get on his motorcycle. I figured I better stick with him—I guess I must have figured I could keep him from getting too fucked up – like in an accident.

I was not wearing a shirt, only a leather vest, and my leather pants and boots. It was late in the summer and getting pretty cool at night. I jumped on the back of the bike and he took off, moving fast.

He was wearing a helmet and couldn't hear a word I was screaming, as I tried to convince him to turn around and go back home. He was having none of that shit. We were heading north on I-75.

We drove and drove, for, like an hour. Finally, just south of the exit off I-75 at Clio, Michigan, he swerved off the freeway, blew through some kind of shit fence and drove the bike out into a field where he dumped it and me in the grass. Then he walked over to a tree, sat down and pulled the helmet over his face.

So I figured, I'm gonna have to call somebody to get me out of here. I'm fucking freezing by this time—remember? No fucking shirt.

I walked a half-mile up to a Shell station at the top of the exit ramp and called my friend, Norm Lyle. It's like, 2:00 in the morning.

He answers the phone at his parents' house and I tell him the story. At this point, he hasn't seen me since I left the party with Schaffer—two hours ago.

He agrees to come pick us up, and he brings his sister, Marty, for the ride. This is an hour and 20 minute drive, he's still stoned, and I figured he needed the company.

Now, they finally arrive in Clio and it's going on 3:30 a.m. I walked Norm out to the field where Brian was. As we walked up to him, sitting under the tree, we could hear him talking. We got up there, pulled his helmet off; turns out he was talking to a fly inside his helmet.

Okay.

Norm and I helped him up, and the three of us began to push his Honda 305 Scrambler across the field, and back to the exit ramp, about a 20 degree incline. By the time we got that fucker to the top of the ramp, we were all exhausted. Completely fucking spent.

Norm knew he was never gonna be able to drive back now; it's 4 a.m. and he's pretty much fucked. His sister didn't have a driver's license, and neither did I.

So guess who drives us back to Birmingham?

Brian Schaffer.

God was definitely watching out for my interests that night.

When we got back to Detroit from Woodstock, we were running loose because we just made a bunch of money. I was becoming more and more incorrigible and my mother was getting very upset with me. We had gone to a party at Mark Weibel's house off Cranbrook Road between Maple Road and Quarton Road.

Now, here's where I go to juvenile hall.

Schaffer told me he wanted me to pick his girlfriend up who lived over by Seaholm. So he gave me the van. Now, I didn't have a driver's license but why would I care? I did what I wanted so I drove that van anyway. I had already driven all the way out to California twice. I might as well just drive around Birmingham, drunk on my ass.

Schaffer told me to go to his mom's house and pick up some "skins" — condoms — and get his girlfriend Kathy, and bring her back to Weibel's house.

Weibel's house was like a zoo because Mark's mother would buy us whiskey and beer and cigarettes. We could do all the drugs and anything we wanted in her home. We thought that was cool. Now you've got to realize, when you look back, that's fucked up that his mother would let us all sit around and get drunk with her. Now, I don't know if she wanted to screw some of us or what her problem was, but she was a wackjob letting kids get drunk and all that other shit.

Anyway, I picked up Brian's necessities for him and some liquor for me. We were driving back to Weibel's house right in front of Seaholm High School. I was talking with Kathy, she had her legs sitting in the middle of the two front seats in a Volkswagen van. I blew through a stop sign while I was talking to her; probably going 40 miles an hour.

Bam! I knew just as I went through the stop sign that I fucked up. I swung the van to the right but I was already on the other side of the road. If I would have gone straight, I would have run straight into Seaholm High School.

I swung to the right and coming at me was a 1969 Mercury Cougar. I smashed, head-on, into the Cougar. I flew out of the van because the windshields popped out of the VW vans then, and landed on the hood of this Cougar. The smoke was pouring out of the hood of the car. I heard kids crying in the car, and the girl who was driving it was evidently the babysitter, and going somewhere. I'd just interrupted their day. This was a fun-filled afternoon for me. NOT!

I was going at a good rate of speed and she was going, you know, on Cranbrook Road, probably 35, 40, I don't know. Anyway, sirens and the cops come. I had gotten off of the hood of the car and I got the little kids out of the car because they were crying. The girl got out. The Birmingham police naturally arrived and asked me for my driver's license, which I couldn't hand over because I didn't have one. So they ran my name and, unbeknownst to me, my mother had put out a complaint with the juvenile authorities to have me taken in as an incorrigible— an uncontrollable child. Because ever since my dad died, I was a bad kid.

The cops took me to the Birmingham Police Station, and my friends happened to be at Shain Park, our local hippie/freak hangout, across the street from the station. They saw what was happening and started spitting at the police for taking me in like some kind of wild revolutionary party for me. Really, it was a goodbye party, they just didn't know that. My friends weren't going to let me go without pushback.

The police took me into the Oakland County Juvenile Home which is basically a total piece of shit prison for kids at the time.

I went before a judge and he committed me, and my mother just took off. She didn't even seem to give two shits.

I didn't see any of this coming. Here I was at a party, and all of a sudden, I'm in juvenile detention. I wasn't going anywhere. They put me in one of these small rooms with a little door that had a little window with wire mesh in it you could look out of. The room was probably an eight foot by eight foot space with a metal bed frame—no mattress during the day. You got your mattress at night, and then you had to lay that down to sleep. In the morning, you checked your mattress back in.

They kept me in solitary confinement my first 14 days or 15 days there. When I was ordered to stand in line, I had to put my feet on the tiles, and there was a line on the tiles. You'd have to count off so they could keep track of everybody, nobody went on the run.

There was this big black guy named Alvin Emory. Now, Alvin was probably 6'3," I don't know — a tall guy. He would stand behind me and flick me behind my ears, calling me "Lily Pad."

I didn't like being in juvenile detention. And this guy was getting on my fucking nerves. Well, I have a very bad temper, and I turned around and I smashed Alvin Emory right in the nose — hit him hard as can be. I knocked him down, and he was a big, big black guy. Well, I had to go stay for an extra 7 to 10 days in solitary confinement for my actions, of course. Because that's what they did then. And the two supervisors we had were Sammy Simms and Tommy Lloyd. Come to find out later, Tommy Lloyd became the director of the whole thing and just retired maybe 10 years ago. He was raised in Oakland County Juvenile Home as a kid, and so was Sammy Simms. They were in there together. Tommy Lloyd had joined the Marines and Sammy had gone off and played for the Kansas City Chiefs for a while. They both eventually came back and worked with the juvenile home where they were raised. They were both in there for neglect when they were kids.

They buddied up to me and I got to be their — I don't know if you'd say their thug, but since I beat that big guy up, they decided when somebody was being an asshole, they would come over and tell me, *Lill, go kick his ass!* This is the juvenile home where you're supposed to be getting better.

Time went on and I got more privileges and they would give me cigarettes. Sammy Simms took me out on New Year's and bought me a bottle of Bali Hai, a cheap wine, and cigarettes. I got to celebrate New Year's Eve 1971 in juvenile detention. I remember Sammy had a Dodge Charger at the time, a hot car. We drank and I was out of the juvenile home for that night. Then he snuck me back in and put me in my cell.

After the car crash, my knee had become infected—the emergency brake had impaled it, and the infection went into my bone. Because of that, they moved me over to a nicer building where I could recover. I was warned to stay off my leg for a couple weeks or else I could lose it. I stayed put.

After a while there, I improved enough to where I could get back on my legs. They moved me to a different room, and soon after another guy was brought in.

He was big—BIG. I'm not exactly sure how tall but I'm only fifteen years old then so he looks like a fucking giant. Definitely a lot bigger than me. Sammy Simms gets a hold of me and tells me, "Now, Lill, be careful with that guy."

I said, "Why, what's the matter? Is he going to beat me up?

He says, "Well, I don't know what he's going to do, but he just murdered both his parents. His name was William Rosen. He killed his father and his mother and tried to make it look like somebody broke in."

Great. Now I'm in here with a fucking killer.

Bill Rosen was kind of a nice guy, actually. I played ping pong with him a bunch but I knew I had to keep an eye on this guy because, hey… he killed his parents. Apparently he shot them both while they were in bed, and then he cut the screen from the inside or something. You know, to make it look like somebody broke in. Anyway, they figured out he did it. He never had to go to trial, I know that. He ended up being placed in Pontiac State Mental Institution, which was still open at the time.

I finally got a little break to go work at the courthouse because Sammy Simms and Tommy Lloyd were taking care of me now. I did them favors when they had problems with other kids who didn't want to join up, so they helped me out in return. When a kid was too much trouble, I got the nod to kick their ass, which I did.

You've got to make yourself comfortable wherever you are. You have to do whatever it takes to make it through, and I quickly learned who was going to help me get through. Sammy and Tommy did that for me. Sammy wore a black leather jacket and Tommy Lloyd was a little short, tough guy with tattoos. Tommy was a former Marine who did a tour in Vietnam, so you can imagine what he was like.

This detention center was not a place for babies. Anyway, I got to working in the print shop for the courthouse so I could walk between there and the children's village. I had free rein at certain times of the day and I could basically do what I wanted, which was kind of cool for me then.

One day I was getting on the elevator, and there was this group of black thugs getting on with me. It turns out they were from a gang called the Black Disciples and they had committed a murder at Oakland Community College. They had raped and killed a girl, and then shot her boyfriend and left him for dead. Somehow, he didn't die and was able to identify all these guys. It was one of the first times in

Michigan that kids were tried as adults.

I knew exactly who they were as they stepped on the elevator, and now I'm thinking, *I've got a murderer who killed his parents for a roommate and I'm riding in elevators with gang members who kill and rape women.* Funny, my mother thought she was fixing me up. She had no idea. Later in life, she read an article about the Oakland County Juvenile Home and how bad it really was. She told me that if she had known what was going on, she would've done something. I said, "Mother, you didn't even know that dad was beating me up, how would you know what was going on in that place?"

Finally, the judge let me go as a wayward minor. My mother went to court and told them I wasn't ready to get out yet, and that I was just going to go back and do what I always did.

Well, the judge wasn't listening to her and he told my mother that if she didn't take me home, he was going to charge her with neglect. All I could think was, *yeah, tell her!* He basically told her that I did everything I was supposed to do, and the courts have done all they can for me. I wanted to get out. I had ulterior motives. I knew I had to go back to my mother's house, but I was going to turn 17 so I could leave home anyway.

I got out of juvenile detention just before my 17th birthday. I had to live a couple of weeks with my mom but I didn't care. Some of my buddies had just rented a farm in Southfield, and had my room ready. I just had to wait a little longer. It was a small farmhouse on maybe a quarter acre off Telegraph Road, south of 13 Mile Road. The second I turned 17, I moved right into the farm.

It was a wild house. Women in and out, tons of drugs. The only thing missing at the time was my hair because it was still short. Part of being in juvenile detention is a clean cut and they scalped me right after I got there.

We had a buddy named Bobby Sirpella. Bobby had opened a store off Northwestern Highway called Cider Mill Village with a guy named Barry Krupp. They sold pipes, boots, incense—all kinds of stuff, and they made candles. Bobby had these 50-gallon drums inside our garage at the farm, and we'd stick our hands in there and make candles and goof off. Bobby was a real cool guy. Schaffer, me, everybody — we were doing way too many drugs. We were into Tuinals, Seconals—Brian was getting into heroin, and things were getting out of hand. We weren't as friendly with each other any more. We fought a lot.

Meantime, Dick Sloss was running around with some new friends he'd made; Rick Marr and Chuck "Chungo" Manko, who was a heroin dealer/pimp on the west side of Detroit. Kind of a piece of shit, but somehow, in his life, he was probably a good guy. You know, everybody is born good. They just go bad along the way. God has a lot to do with it. I have friends say to me, *Oh, so you've found Jesus.* No, I didn't find Jesus. God found me. I was just a mess. I was doing too many drugs, and things were getting too crazy.

Brian and I went to a party at Sloss' house when his parents were out of town. We were all eating Tuinals, everybody was falling and banging around. One night, Schaffer and I got into a knock-down fight over some small thing because we were eating so many tuinals. We might have killed each other if Dick's brother Jim and another friend, Norm Lyle, hadn't broken up the fight. We smashed out a pantry door in the Sloss kitchen.

We were really getting into just making money so we would cut anything. We were selling PCP— shit, we sold anything people would buy. We even sold LSD that had strychnine in it—orange wedge. They were going around. I didn't care for that, didn't want to sell that shit. But Schaffer was getting unpredictable. Those orange wedges would make you sick, but it would also make you hallucinate.

In the words of Iggy Pop, it was "no fun."

People didn't care whether or not it was pure LSD any more. This is about the time that the whole idea of rock and roll and being hippies was dying. You know, it sounds crazy but we had some kind of code of morality for a while. We cared about our customers — the hippie way of life.

At some point, though, it became all about the money. More money brought on more problems. Schaffer was doing heroin, and I was getting pissed. I could see it all falling apart.

One night, I went down to Schaffer's basement at his parents' house, and he was with a girlfriend of his, Kathy. They were sitting there still tied off with needles dangling out of their arms. Brian said, "Come on in, do some Jones." *I don't want to do any fucking Jones.*

Finally, Schaffer and Larry got me to try it one time and it made me puke. According to them, it was good Jones if it makes you throw up. Well, I was drinking and doing a lot of shit then, but to me, if it makes you puke, I don't want it. I'll stick to drinking. Schaffer got into it. Dickie was way into it, and he started losing his shit. Everything was getting crazy. Everything was going bad and heroin was involved. Heroin, heroin, heroin. I knew something bad was bound to happen.

We moved into a place with Woody Keane about 1971. Woody was the guy we were smuggling hash for that was hidden in puzzles. Well, this place was in Farmington Hills — a condominium subdivision. Brian and I had already been falling apart — not seeing things eye to eye, I guess you could say. We moved in with Woody and his wife, Meg. We were doing PCP, Brian was selling heroin, and I was still trying to sell pot but also some harder drugs.

Schaffer wanted to go out on this one night in August of '71. He said he had a new girlfriend and he really liked her. He didn't want to mess this up.

I said, "Well, Brian, don't be doing heroin and screwing up when you take her out tonight." I stayed back at the apartment and just wanted to lay back and do some drugs with Woody and Meg. Woody was about eight or nine years older than us, but he liked working with us because we hustled hard. We had to if we wanted to impress the older crowd. We thought we were hot shots, hanging out with older guys. Everybody thought they were way cool. But really, we were all just stupid.

Anyway, I shake hands with Schaffer and I don't know why, but I had this feeling I wasn't going to see him again. I said, "Be careful, don't get screwed up, treat this girl nice if you like her that much. Don't show her how we are." He said, "Be cool, I will."

Then he left.

At about one o'clock in the morning, the phone rings. I answer the phone and it's Beaumont Hospital asking if it was the residence of a Brian Schaffer. I said, "Yeah". The person on the phone said, "Well, he's been killed in a car accident."

Oh, shit. Brian is dead. Just like that.

Looking back, I knew things were starting to go real bad with all the drugs and the alcohol. See, when you're drinking and doing drugs, you're not paying attention in the moment. You lose sight of things.

And all your friends — I mean, everybody — is splitting up because they're more focused on the next high. I knew things were not going right but I continued to stay in the circle.

We weren't really friends anymore, just using each other for the convenience and the drugs. I did a little cocaine before Brian died, not much. But after he died, I got into it really heavily. It almost killed me, but in an indirect way, it also saved my life.

Drinking and drugs, they all lead to the same road — either you're going to die or your friends are going to die. It's not a pretty life. God is working through me to reach anyone struggling with drugs and addiction. If I say 'God' too much for you, I haven't said it enough, because He can help you.

When I lost Brian, I was broken-hearted. I didn't know what to do so I did the only thing I knew and started eating a lot of Tuinals and Seconals. I went off the deep end. I went to Beaumont Hospital and saw him underneath the sheet. There's something surreal about seeing your best friend lying on a table under a sheet. It's him but it's not him. It doesn't feel completely real, but the little bit that does feel real hurts. I wanted to wipe out that "realness," I wanted that memory, that feeling, gone.

So I split. I actually had a bag of Tuinals in my pocket. I was wearing my leather pants and I remember thinking that I could eat them and forget about what I just saw, or I could take a step in the other direction. I threw those Tuinals all over the parking lot. I broke the bag open. I never took another Tuinal again in my life. Brian's death actually saved my life.

Sometimes I talk like I'm mad, and I guess I kind of am mad. I'm mad that I got fucked up with Brian and, even after his death, I still hadn't learned yet. Even though I threw out those drugs in the parking lot that night, I still wasn't seeing clearly. With that one step forward, two steps backward weren't far off. I wasn't seeing straight.

Yet.

CHAPTER TWO

Cocaine

Even though Brian had the connections with who we bought our drugs from, I knew them all. Guys like Matthew Locricchio, Tommy Swanson, Woody Keane, and numerous older guys typically did business with Brian, but I figured I better get back in the game and start making money again.

I needed a way to recover from his death. I went through some serious bouts of depression and I was taking a lot of Nembutols and Seconols. I tried to kill myself a couple of times. Each time I ended up at Beaumont Hospital and they pumped my stomach. When I got out, I just carried on and went back to drinking more Boone's Farm and Orange Smash. Those were the drinks I liked.

And of course beer.

And vodka.

Hell, anything, I guess. That's a true alcoholic, for ya. A good old-fashioned alcoholic. Soon I was mixing the booze with pills.

Mixing uppers with downers is fucking stupid.

Anyway, Larry Bergland and I started running together and we're partners again. I was living with Woody Keane, Brian's dead, the whole thing is a mess.

Larry had a sister named Christine. His other sister was in a folk band called The Princess and the Frog. Now, The Princess and the Frog was a male and female folk group; they played at the Raven Gallery on Greenfield Road. They met Josh White, Jr., who was a well-known black folk singer, at the club. He hooked up with Christine, Larry's sister and, you know, in the 70s, living with a black man wasn't very popular, especially with her parents. So she moved to New York and hung out with Josh there. He was a star. He still is today, in fact. His father, Josh White, Sr., was also a pretty famous folk singer.

Josh had some kids in New York with another woman, but she lived in Harlem, which was a very tough place, even then. You didn't want to find yourself down there alone, especially alone and white. Josh lived outside of Harlem in a penthouse, and Chrissy lived with him.

Anyway, his wife was missing and he wanted to go to her apartment in Harlem and have somebody stay at his penthouse with Chrissy. He paid me and Larry to come out to New York and go to his wife's place in Harlem to clean out this apartment. Josh knew something wasn't right with the situation, but he didn't exactly tell us what it was.

I didn't care; I was game for anything at this point in my life. I had dead friends — things were falling apart big time in the Motor City for me. So I thought, What the hell? I was always ready for adventure, trust me. If you said there was a million dollars in a room with 40 people guarding it, I would try to get it if you asked me to. I liked doing risky shit, which is another word for stupid shit, but for money you could have me.

So Josh took us to New York to stay at his apartment. When it came time to go down into Harlem and check out her apartment, I didn't think anything of it. I was just helping out a friend, right?

We get to Harlem and, I mean, it's just like "Harlem Nights." They're dancing in the street, sitting on cars, and we're white. We walk through the apartment building, and there's people sitting on the stairs, sitting in cars, all black people mind you. But they kind of embraced us because we had Josh White with us, and he's black. So we go upstairs, check out the apartment. Larry's sister goes in one room, she's cleaning out drawers. A couple of minutes later she comes walking out with this big Ziploc bag full of white powder. Larry and I—I mean, we're druggies, okay? And we look at that and just think, Woah!

She said, "Do you guys know what this is? Should I throw it out?"

I said I would take a look at it first. You know, see what it actually is. Larry and I each dip our fingers in it and taste it, and it's pure cocaine. I know the taste of cocaine very well by now. If you've ever tasted cocaine in your life you'll know what I mean when I say that it had that special freeze taste.

We told her we could sell it, but she wanted to throw it out. We jumped and said, "DON'T THROW THAT SHIT OUT! This is worth a lot of money." It was maybe three-quarters of a pound, I'm not sure exactly because we never did weigh it. We had every intention of selling it but we ended up shooting most of it when we got back to Detroit.

Back then, you could fly without any worries at all. Just stuff any kind of shit in your pockets and walk on a plane. Nobody checked you for shit, okay? So we just flew it home, decided we were going to come back to Detroit and be big cocaine dealers. Well, it didn't really work out that way. We did sell a bit of it, but we started shooting it and then it was game over.

Once you start shooting cocaine, you just need more. I would shoot huge amounts and my ears would ring, so I would shoot more to get that ring back in my ears. Man, my arms had tracks up and down. I had to wear long sleeve shirts. A couple of times I got what you call an abscess, which became infected. I went back to my old doctor, Dr. Dorsey, who had treated me for encephelitis when I was a kid.

He lanced it for me and the infection went away. I could have lost my arm because abscesses are very dangerous. Not only that, but I contracted serum hepatitis, or hepatitis B, by using dirty needles. We did sell a little bit of the cocaine, gave a little more to girls to look cool and, ultimately, put the rest into our own veins. We both came out of the situation with no cocaine, no money, and hepatitis.

Even with hepatitis, Larry continued to get high and drink. I had a friend, Dale Ott, whose mother let me recuperate at her house. I laid up sick for weeks and I knew I wasn't going to get over hepatitis B by partying so I got the fuck out of Detroit.

My mother lived in Florida at this time, so I asked her if I could come stay long enough to get well. She agreed and I bought a plane ticket to Sarasota. I stayed on my mom's couch for about six months while working at getting healthier. That worked fine except one thing: everybody in Detroit knew where I was. My friends, Bill Whitney and John Halebian, had come down to the Keys for a visit, and they were on their way back to Detroit. I was feeling better, but I was ready to get out and get back to making money. She said, "So, you're going back up there again?" Yeah. Well, I didn't learn anything; I had to go back. I was going to go back and be a drug dealer. Of course my mother was mad. Why wouldn't she be? I mean, I basically used her until I felt better and then left on my merry way.

Halebian and Whitney picked me up and we started making our way toward Michigan, but we decided to stop in Cartersville, Georgia. Halebian knew this guy named Leroy, a barber who also happened to be in the Ku Klux Klan. We're hippies, right — well, more like rock 'n rollers. Our hair hung down our backs, we wore leather pants and jackets. To a small-town Georgian, we looked like hippies. There were no flowers in our hair, if you know what I mean. We fought our way through life, we didn't hold our arms out and sway in the breeze, right?

Cartersville, Georgia is a very small town. Everybody knew everybody. Leroy was building an apartment complex and he wanted us to help him out. He paid us $3 an hour in cash and he let us live in one of the apartments. I painted — they started calling me 'Painter Boy' — and Halebian and Whitney both had some carpentry skills.

One day we heard that some of my Detroit friends, the Francavillas, got transferred to Georgia for the carpet business they owned and operated. They were headed to Chambliss, which is about three hours from Cartersville. We thought it was a good idea to go visit Bobby and Carl Francavilla one night. Bobby and Carl had made some friends in their new high school and, well, needless to say these guys were pretty redneck-y.

Remember that Whitney, Halebian and me, well, we looked like Yankees from Detroit. *Up North.* We listened to rock and roll; the MC5, The Stooges—we went to the Grande Ballroom, right? In Chambliss, Georgia, they listened to country music. You know, "Georgia On My Mind" and shit.

Bobby Francavilla heard about a hotel party that was sure to have booze and girls, so we went along with them. It had been awhile since I'd really partied and you better believe I was ready to get back at it. When we walked into this room, the girls just looked at us like we were from outer space. They were used to camo-wearin', gun-totin' rednecks. Here we come with our long hair, tight leather pants, and rock-n-roll attitudes.

It was intriguing for them. We were something different, and we were damn sure going to capitalize on that game. It's probably no surprise to anybody that the local guys didn't like their girls paying attention to us whatsoever. We grabbed beers from a bathtub full of ice and started talking to some people.

Everything seemed to be going okay and then this girl started being friendly, like, very friendly toward me. I'm sitting on the end of the bed and I start thinking to myself, *I'm about to pick this girl up!* There are about 20 people in this room and, you know, not a lot of seating, so I didn't think anything of another guy sitting against the headboard. You got to sit somewhere, right?

Well this guy, Billy, throws a rolled up cigarette pack at me just to annoy me. I didn't pay attention to that because I'm focused on this girl so I just continued talking to her again. Apparently the empty cigarette pack didn't get enough attention out of me so Billy threw a beer can and it hit me in the head — a full beer can.

That pissed me off.

I stood up at the end of the bed, turned around and just looked at the guy. As he stood, he took a few steps closer to me and said, "What are you going to do?"

I didn't say a word; everything in my mind just went blank. He provoked me and I was mad. The only thing I could think to do was take a swing. In a room where we were outnumbered, I did exactly that. I punched him square in the face.

Bad move.

The room had already been quiet as soon as the exchange began, but when I swung on that guy, the silence became suffocating. Everybody in the room turned against the three of us — me, Whitney and Halebian. Someone broke a lamp and held the jagged base against Whitney's neck where he had been standing in one corner of the room.

Another group used their elbows and knees and pinned Halebian against the wall in another corner of the room, and everybody else turned toward me.

I knew in that moment I wasn't going to get backup from my buddies. They weren't going to struggle against the rednecks, and I don't blame them for it. It's not like they deserted me, they were told to stay out of it.

At this point, the girls were encouraging Billy and rallying him on, saying shit like, "Kill him, Billy! Kill him! Kick his ass!" Some other guys who weren't already pinning Whitney and Halebian up took their belts off and wrapped them around their hands with the belt buckles on their knuckles. They beat the shit out of me.. I mean I got hurt bad. I can't say how long this went on but long enough for someone to hear the screaming and security to run through the door. I started hearing and seeing the scene around me in a distant, muffled way. I thought I was dead, or at least on my way there.

After security came in, the police were called. After the typical questioning, the cops called an ambulance because I was really in a bad way. I wasn't too keen on an ambulance so I told them I wasn't going to the hospital, I'd be fine. My buddies helped me out of the hotel and to the car. Each step was as painful as another punch with those homemade knuckles.

Before we left, the cops had asked if I wanted to press charges and, even though my face was smashed in and I had busted ribs, I wouldn't do it. I just wanted out of that place. I later found out that all those guys beating me were killed in alcohol-related accidents of one kind or another.

Mrs. Francavilla took care of me for quite a while at the Francavilla house until I could recover because I could barely even walk on my own.

As soon as I was well enough to drive, the three of us went back to Detroit. We wanted nothing to do with Georgia. We hit the road and didn't even look back. I was going back to living the life I've always lived in Detroit, but little did I know it would be short-lived. My next business opportunity would take me to the west coast — The Golden State of California.

When I returned to Michigan from Georgia, I had heard Larry Bergland was still shooting cocaine and heroin. He wasn't even trying to get over the hepatitis. Eventually Larry died due to liver failure from chronic hepatitis. When I heard that I had lost another friend to drug and alcohol abuse, all those same feelings ran over me again. He was another fallen angel.

So, when I was in Detroit, I decided to visit my brother Mike, who was living downtown near Alexandrine and Woodward. I hadn't seen him in like, 4 years.

It was an old Victorian apartment building that had been remodeled so there were now apartments in the basement area. It was one of these apartments Mike was living in.

Bill Whitney, Norm Lyle and I went down to see Mike.

When we got there and knocked on his door, we were fucking startled when he answered the door.

Mike had grown a pretty good beard, but it was all pushed up on one side; like he'd been sleeping on it for days—maybe he had.

He was wearing a slightly tattered woman's red nightgown, but otherwise, no shoes, no slippers—no nothing.

The place was a mess. Just a simple one room apartment, with kitchen and bath. Trash and garbage, in boxes and paper bags—this is in the days when plastic garbage bags were just appearing—lined the outside walls up to a height of maybe three feet!

In the middle of the room was a filthy, two inch thick mattress; around this mattress stood, maybe, 30 empty bottles of cheap bourbon. An ashtray sat there with a fucking mountain of ashes and cigarette butts. As we talked, Mike kept picking up the empty bottles and tipping them over his mouth to extract the last few, precious, life-enhancing drops of cheap bourbon. It was like watching a comedy about drunks.

We talked for some time and finally I went about trying to help clean up, even if just a little. His toilet was clogged and there were dirty dishes in the sink. After a few grueling minutes, I had completed these unpleasant tasks when I noticed mouse or rat droppings in one of his kitchen drawers.

I pointed this out to Mike, and he explained that this was his "pet mouse." Wait…what?!

I'm looking at this fucking hell-hole my brother is living in, and he's telling me about his pet mouse!

I got pissed off and said to Mike, "That's no pet! Show me this mouse and I'll kill it!"

It was like all the air had been sucked out of the room. A real dark look came over Mike's face, and he glared at me like he didn't know me any longer.

"Nobody is gonna kill my pet mouse!" he screamed and he picked up a carving knife from the kitchen—one I had just cleaned. He held it under my chin and repeated himself.

I figured Whitney and Lyle were discussing letting the brothers work this out for themselves when I slipped away from Mike and we all ran our asses out of there.

For many years, that was the last image I had of my brother Mike; chasing us east down Alexandrine as we drove off in Lyle's car, swinging that carving knife in the air, and dressed in that red nightgown. You should surely know that alcohol and mental illness do not mix!

Understand, I'm not condemning the responsible use of alcohol… I am asking those who have lost control of their use of alcohol and any other substances, to quit. You are worth it!

God Bless.

I got my shit together, and looked up a couple of the old drug dealing pals, Tommy Swanson and Matthew Locricchio. Naturally, they were still doing their thing, and doing really well. I mean, why quit when you're a high roller? They had great apartments in an affluent area in Troy. I wanted to start selling again so Tommy and Matthew would front me PCP to push for them.

I still had a market to move PCP, mescaline, and LSD, but it wasn't the good LSD and it wasn't the good mescaline anymore. Everybody was buffing stuff out, putting speed in it. Drugs were getting bad, okay? That sounds like an oxymoron, but the truth is, drugs that were laced with speed were getting more dangerous.

Tom told me he was moving to Mill Valley, California with his old lady, Bonnie, who was pregnant. Tom always had money because he was a major outlet in Detroit, and he knew a bunch of chemists in San Francisco making PCP. He had connections and I wanted in. He asked me if I wanted to come out there with him so I could work for him and bring some back to Detroit. I'd be a runner, a mule.

Of course I said yes. I mean, I didn't have anything else to do and I lived for adventure. Plus, everybody was fucking dead. Hell, I still needed to make money and I've always been a capitalist at heart.

We had neighbors around there who were "somebodies," you know what I mean? People, like, from Jefferson Airplane. Grace Slick and David Crosby were living around there then. Mill Valley was only about six miles from Sausalito and we would head over there to hang out. I thought I was a big shot, living with a drug dealer in a beautiful house, hanging out near big musicians, watching them out and about. Hell, I'd see David Crosby riding around town on his motorcycle now and then. I didn't have a care in the world surrounded by beaches, drugs, and money. I was loving life in California. I had this "Enjoy Cocaine" T-shirt, long hair, and a badass pair of snakeskin boots. I mean, I was cool and I was flying back and forth to Detroit selling PCP.

After a while we decided we wanted to start tabbing it. Tommy bought a tabbing machine. He found a 1948 model that was only good for making loud *ker-clunk* noises. We go to some tool and die place, and this guy makes parts for it. It's up and running, and we started tabbing the PCP into little pink tabs.

We code named them Pink Fuck. My job was to continue taking product back to Detroit, so I flew Pink Fuck to Detroit, and I was making an okay living doing that.

I guess Tommy wanted to expand our reach, so to say, so he asked me if I knew anybody in Florida. Other than my mom—who I knew wasn't interested—I didn't know anyone, but I told him I'd go anyway.

I went to the airport in Detroit and I bought a ticket to Daytona Beach. I don't know why I picked Daytona. I guess you could say I just threw the proverbial dart and it hit Daytona Beach. Since Tommy was financing this scouting trip, I didn't care where I went. Because you weren't that paranoid back then. Back then, you could walk up to people and start talking about drugs. It's a lot different now. You can't do that kind of shit.

I had a small suitcase and I put a couple thousand PCPs in it and I threw in some black Pakistani hash that I picked up in Detroit. So I jumped on the airplane to Florida with my suitcase full of PCP.

I found my seat in coach — it's not like I was flying First Class, or anything — and I settled in for the short flight to Florida. As I'm starting to relax, I feel a light tap on my shoulder. I turn around and see a beautiful girl smiling at me.

I said hello.

She said hello.

I'm still wondering what the hell is going on. Her name is Brenda and she asked me to come sit in the empty seat next to her. This is during a time when you could just switch your seat if you wanted to. Nobody gave a shit.

I gathered my things and sat next to her. She asked me what I was doing in Florida because, obviously, she knew I was heading there. We're both on a flight to Daytona. I said, "I know I'm moving to Daytona Beach, but I don't know where yet." This chick jumps right into, "Do you know where to get any good drugs in Detroit? Did you bring any?" Of course I'm going to bite and I said, "Yeah, I have some THC." This was a time when we sold PCP as THC. I told her I had some that I wanted to get rid of and I was going to sell it in Daytona. Brenda told me that her boyfriend, Ben, could help me. He sold pot and LSD. This is how loose the world was back then. I was drinking cocktails on the airplane and I'm only 19 years old. I'm wearing my "Enjoy Cocaine" t-shirt, snakeskin wristbands that I had made out of anaconda skin when I was out west, and my hair is hanging long. I looked like a hippy, but I looked like I had money. Well, I did, actually. I didn't look like a bum.

We landed in Daytona Beach, and Brenda wanted to take me straight to Ben. I went to her house and met Ben. He's cool and we hit it off. Ben told me I could stay there. I showed him my PCP pills — THC — and he said he could get rid of all of them. He knew people he could sell them to. Ben was a bartender and bartenders know where to get rid of things. And in those days, he knew all the biker bars, he knew everybody. I thought, Bingo, I'm in.

I stayed with them for a while but then I wanted to get my own place, because I was going to strip clubs and I was making money. I told Tommy, I got a hold of him, and I said we can get rid of a lot of THC in this town. He was the boss. Tommy was, like, 29, 30 years old and Bonnie, his old lady, was pregnant.

Now here's another time I should have stepped in and I didn't. Tommy used to beat Bonnie regularly, and I didn't do anything about it.

To be honest, I was used to seeing people get beat up. I just thought it was part of life. I'd just say to myself, Poor Bonnie, and move on. Time and again, I watched her go right back to him twenty minutes after he gave her a black eye, and I'd say to myself, Poor Bonnie, and move on. I'm not proud of sitting back and letting that happen. I'd do things differently today.

Ben gets going in the THC business and he actually starts getting pretty well-known. Indirectly, people knew me because they all heard he was hanging around with this guy from Detroit. Yours truly, little me with long hair.

It was known that I wouldn't work with anybody else, so no one would approach me. Ben was my guy and Brenda was his old lady. I had a good thing going. In fact, it was so good that I had two apartments on the beach, the Marco Polo and the Polynesian Inn.

I kept my pills in one and my money in another.

Here I am supplying all of Daytona Beach with THC. After I bought a gram of THC and buffed it out, I'd go back to California, stay up all night for three or four days and tab up. We'd tab bunches of it up.

Bonnie was a seamstress and she would get these big stuffed animals to use as a way to transport the pills. But I didn't travel with the stuffed animals. Some hippie kid flying with a big stuffed animal might look a little suspicious. I took risks but I wasn't stupid. The process included Bonnie mailing the stuffed animals to Daytona and I'd pick them up a few days after I landed, sell all the pills, then send the money back to Tommy.

It worked and I kept running around for a while until Ben approached me and asked if I could get him one big batch of 10,000. He said he could sell it all at once. I said, "Well, yeah, I think I can." The only catch was, I would have to front it to him. It was above my pay grade to give him an answer right then and there. That's a lot of money at a buck a hit — a $10,000 deal. Ten grand was a big deal in the seventies.

I started seeing dollar signs and I was pretty confident Tommy would go for it. He was all about making money, and making money quick was even better. So I called Tommy. Tommy's seeing dollar signs because we could make up to 1,500 single tabs out of one gram of the crystal. At $300 a gram, we were standing to profit a lot of money..

Tommy and I got to work on the tabbing machine.

Ker-clunk, ker-clunk. Cha-ching, cha-ching.

Anyhow, I set the deal up. Ben says he's got this guy named Bob Ruhl who owns a car wash in Daytona Beach. He's, like, the local businessman, but he's a drug dealer. Bob the Businessman wears nice slacks, shirt, tie, and he ran the local car wash directly across the street from the Marco Polo Hotel where I was staying.

He arranged to make a deal and said that he was going to do it on a Saturday at his car wash. I gave the pills to Ben who gave the pills to Bob Ruhl. Bob Ruhl gave the pills to a guy named Steve who worked for him and had set this deal up. My cut was five grand which was a lot of money for a kid. I was rolling. I thought I was the big shit, to be honest with you.

As the time approaches for the deal, I'm sitting in my room at the Marco Polo. That's where I kept my drugs but, by then, I had pretty much gotten rid of most of them.

So I'm on pins and needles waiting for the phone call to pick up my money. I turn on the TV to kill some time and settle on the afternoon news. As I'm watching a live shot taking place in Daytona Beach, I notice a Corvette parked at a carwash and rolled up on the hood of the car is a denim jacket — *my denim jacket!* I used my jacket to wrap the pills in and I'm sitting in my hotel room watching this unfold on live TV.

The cops are everywhere, and the journalist is reporting a big drug seizure. It took me all of two minutes to jump into action and get my things packed to get the hell out of there. Hell, they were just across the street. All I had to do was look out of the hotel window and I could watch the whole thing go down.

I peeked outside and noticed the cops were still there. Now, Bob Ruhl didn't know my name, so I figured I had a few minutes to get out. My heart was pounding. I grab my bags, I get the rest of my pills, and I'm going to check out and get the fuck out of Dodge. I haven't even thought about where I'm going to go exactly, but I know it's nowhere near this shit.

God was with me on this day because as I walk into the front lobby, I see cops — detectives — speaking with the front desk manager. As I'm walking for what feels like miles to get through this lobby, I can see how events could unfold in an unfavorable way. Just keep walking. Be calm.

The manager and I make eye contact. That's it. It's over. They got me.

I keep walking because I'm now on autopilot, right? I kept thinking they would notice me somehow. Maybe I'm walking loudly, maybe they can hear how hard my heart is beating, maybe they can smell the fear. I don't know, but I'm nervous as shit.

For some out-of-this-world reason, that manager let me walk on through without flinching. He knew who I was and yet he didn't say a word to those detectives. I kept my head down through the front doors and jumped in a cab that was waiting nearby. I told the cabbie to take me to Cocoa Beach because Lonnie Gleason, a friend of mine, lived near there. I asked the driver to stop at a pay phone and I called Lonnie. I told him that I was in trouble, I needed a place to crash, and that I had some more of that THC that I needed to dump on my way out of Daytona. I just went straight to his house in Titusville. An hour later, I got out of the cab, paid the fare, and walked up to my next adventure.

My mind is still reeling as I make the trek up to Lonnie's front door. He has a cool little surfer beach house. It's fitting because surfing was Lonnie's profession. That and selling drugs. I barely knocked on the door before it swung open and Lonnie welcomed me in, along with the suitcase of pills and money I still had left. I catch Lonnie up on what went down in Daytona, and the plan for the night is to come up with a plan to get rid of the pills. We decided to get rid of the rest of the pills, and Lonnie insists that we stash them outside. At this point, I don't give a shit. Besides, it's his house so whatever he wants is fine with me. I just needed a place to crash for a night.

We chilled and watched TV that evening and the drug bust in Daytona was still getting plenty of air time. The reporter announced that the police were still looking for one man in connection to the case—yours truly. Lonnie said, "Boy, you're lucky, Jerry."

I replied, unbelievingly, "I know, man," but, really, I don't believe in luck. I don't believe in coincidences either. What I believe in is fate and the life I lived was meant to be shared so anyone reading can learn from me. Learn from my choices and make choices that make more sense for a lifetime of positivity. I'm not saying there weren't some positive times in my life because I had a lot. I'm just saying that some of the choices I made placed obstacles in my path that didn't need to be there.

The next morning I'm in and out of sleep as my body starts to wake up, partly dreaming about the events that unfolded the day before, partly thinking about what I'm going to do to get myself out of this situation. I hear the birds chirping, the rumble of a trash truck, and Lonnie fumbling around in the kitchen.

So I drag myself out of bed because I need to get busy digging myself out of this mess. I need food first, so I walk to the kitchen and eat a quick breakfast. Lonnie said he was going out back to get the pills so we could figure out what to do with them. You know, I never really understood why he wanted them outside. It's not like they would attract mice or anything.

Anyway, remember when I mentioned the trash truck? Well, guess where Lonnie hid the pills. With the fucking trash.

This is about the moment when I realize the PCP I'm selling is cursed. Bad things have gone down ever since I started selling this shit. Lonnie looks at me with "fuck" written all over his face. "So what are we going to do, Lonnie?"

He decided to call the trash company since they were just there and dispatch could track the truck down pretty easily. He called and explained that there were some important papers out there and they took the wrong trash. They believed him, or pretended to, I don't know. Maybe they get calls like that all the time.

We drove to the landfill and they showed us where that particular truck had just dumped. We are walking in trash — disgusting, stinks-like-rot trash — up to our knees. Have you ever been to a landfill? It's all seagulls, shit, and smell. We combed through that heap for hours and, believe it or not, we found a bag of over a thousand of my pills. I knew there was another one but this was enough for me, so we left. Once we got back to Lonnie's house, he sold some of it and said he'd sell the rest when he could. He assured me he would send me the money. I ended up buying some marijuana off him, but he still owed me some money. I didn't want to wait around for that. I told him I was heading to Sarasota and I jumped on the next bus heading to the Gulf Coast.

Although my mother lives in Sarasota, I can't admit to her that I'm in trouble again. I'm not willing to see her disappointment. I do have a cousin who also lives in Sarasota, so I get in touch with Janet.

Janet lives off North 41, over towards the airport. She had a really nice house on Panama Street and I head that way. When I arrived at Janet's house I told her that I thought I was in trouble and just needed a place to hide out for a bit. She allowed me to stay with her even though I really wasn't sure if the cops knew my name or not.

I wasn't sure if Ben had snitched on me, and if the cops knew who I was, they could find me. If not, I just needed time to figure out my next move. The first move I made was to call Tommy Swanson. I explained what happened and he said, "Well, we can do it again. We'll just send you somewhere else."

Are you fucking kidding me?

I stood up to him and I said, "No. I don't want to do that again."

There was just something about that PCP — it had bad energy.

"I'm out, Tommy. I quit," I said. "Not sure what I'm going to do, but I'm not doing that. I can sell pot or something, but I can't sell the pills anymore." Too many things went wrong with pills and chemicals, and we're really not selling THC, we're selling PCP. Angeldust is made out of PCP. It's dangerous as hell. It's 100% an anti-brain drug and I'm surprised my brain still works because I liked it back in the day.

Anyway, I stayed on Janet's couch for a while. I'm still hanging around because, don't forget, Lonnie owes me money.

Janet's got a guy named Bill Pendola and a guy named Russ living with her. Russ has some kind of engineering business and Bill Pendola is a carpenter part-time. Full time, he's a school teacher. Janet is a hippie who sews and bakes, whatever. It's a pretty laid-back place but, soon, these other guys are wondering what I'm doing just hanging around and whether or not I'm going to work and chip in. I actually didn't feel like I needed to work because I already had money.

Well, Bill didn't see it that way. He told me my money would run out and then suggested I work for his dad who built homes for a company out of Detroit. His dad was a framer and the head carpenter for Richmond Homes.

Now, I had never worked in construction in my life, but Bill told me I could just work on Saturdays and get the lay of the land as I learn carpentry. I didn't have anything to do and I was getting bored so I thought, okay, I'll try that.

This turned out to be a great decision because I worked as a carpenter later in life. I always found a sense of satisfaction when I built something with my hands. It was one of the best decisions I made as a young man because it provided me the opportunity to earn an honest living later in life.

I started working for Mr. Pendola on Saturdays, and I didn't even know how to swing a hammer so I knew this was going to be interesting. Mr. Pendola was a short, little, mean old Italian guy. He was a damn good carpenter and, despite his size, he was fast and strong. He drove a blue van, drank a shit-ton of coffee, and only knew how to say "fuck," "get the fuck out," "fuck," and "what the fuck are you doing?"

He was a man of few (colorful) words, if you know what I mean.

I started to admire this guy. Maybe it was because he was the first man who actually taught me a skill, I don't know. The only thing I learned from my old man was how to drink and avoid a beating. And the only skills I learned from drug dealers were how to sell drugs without getting caught. Not exactly a lifelong skill.

Because I was the rookie, the low man on the totem pole, my first job was to put up furring strips. After a few days of nailing furring strips to a block wall with cut nails, I had more blisters than I could count. He was an old-fashioned dude and didn't want to use the nail guns that had just come out to market. He would say, "Why the fuck would I want that when we can hammer 'em in by hand?" He was the meanest sucker but had a great influence on me. He was the reason for how I could get along later in life. Other "apprentices" often quit because their hands hurt so bad. I started wrapping my hands in gauze and medical tape to take the pressure off the blisters. I didn't quit. I kept going.

Mr. Pendola approached me after a couple weeks and told me I had what it takes to be a carpenter. He knew I could take his shit. Hell, he watched me take it day in and day out with taped and bleeding hands. I was determined and noticed improvement after a few months. I was getting good and I actually enjoyed it. Eventually, like all construction jobs, it ended.

Throughout the months I stayed in Sarasota, I met a lot of people. Lonnie Gleason also sent me some Jamaican marijuana because he owed me money. I didn't mind that he was repaying me with marijuana because I could easily sell it. I had thousands of dollars again from working construction and selling the pot. I felt good about myself. I had practical skills from learning construction with Mr. Pendola, Lonnie had paid his debt, and I was getting to know people. Settle in a bit, you know?

I started working for a company called Innis Builders and they were building a big house on the road before you go over to Longboat Key called the Penner house. The owner, Barry Innis, liked to drink. In fact, I later learned that he was a manic-depressive who liked to drink. Not a good combination. I showed up for work one day at the Penner house and the supervisor said we weren't working there that day. Turned out that Barry blew his brains out in his office the night before and the supervisor knew of another gig at the Columbia Restaurant on St. Armand's Circle.

Casey Gonzmart's family owned the restaurant and Casey was a manager. He was maybe 23 or 24 — a young guy. I'm close to his age and, eventually, we really hit it off. Before Barry killed himself, he had signed a contract with Casey to remodel part of the interior of the Columbia Restaurant. The Gonzmarts had already given Barry a lot of money to get started on this job, so what are they going to do now? Casey didn't know what to do because Barry's crew that showed up were lazy and not motivated to get the job done. I had picked up some decent framing skills and I worked hard. It must've shown because Casey asked me if I could help him finish the job.

I said, "Well, yeah. Sure, I'll help you." You know by now that I'm always ready for a new challenge. I was a pretty decent framer by this point. So I took the job and Casey was the boss. He let me hire some other guys and we finished that job. I even made a stained glass door for him, which hung on that Columbia restaurant for quite a long time. It turned out to be a really nice-looking restaurant bar.

Casey was pleased with my work and offered me a job to be the permanent maintenance guy for him. I thought it would be nice to hang around Sarasota and I took the job. . I bought a VW van, my own tools, and worked hard for Casey. I'm working at the Columbia, I had my shit together, I was young and strong, things were going well for me. Casey and I quickly became best friends because we had similar work ethics and were close in age. He was a good dude and helped me get established as a young guy.

You know, I wish I would have stayed there when I look back. I also wish I could say Casey and I are still friends, but my greed soon took over again. Things happened between us and, because of that, I'm sorry. Sometimes you just can't control your destiny.

CHAPTER THREE

Money For Nothing

After I finished working the Columbia Restaurant job, I decided to hang around for a while. I had already met some people and made friends, settled into the area. It was comfortable, you know? Things happen when you stop looking for it to happen, or when you let your guard down.

In the past my guard was always up — it had to be — because my lifestyle was sink or swim. Eat or be eaten. Good things happen when you're least expecting it. As I was hanging out around Lido Beach, I met Janice VanFleet. She was a young, beautiful Cherokee woman from Owensboro, Kentucky. I mean, as pretty and beautiful as you could imagine. Janice was a good girl.

She and her girlfriend, Kathy, who recently died from alcohol poisoning, hung around down at the Sandcastle on Lido Beach, and I used to go there for the drinks, sun, and women. I had decent money since I had worked at the Columbia Restaurant so I could afford to just kick back for the time. Janice and I really hit it off right away, and she quickly became an important part of my life. We spent all of our time together and eventually moved into a place in Sarasota together.

In the interim, I met a guy named Jerry Wojack who was from Detroit and—you guessed it—a drug dealer. In fact, Richard Chosid—my attorney— was his attorney too! Jerry had a house right at the end of Lido Beach, and he had a lot of people coming in and out from Detroit. He owned some kind of boutique up in Detroit, and I wanted to get in with those guys because he was talking about some people I knew — including Matthew Locricchio.

My drug-dealing, demented mind started reeling and I thought I could get something out of this. I was always up to making money and I was a hustler. Just down the street from my place with Janice was Walt's Fish Market, which was a tiny little white building down 301. Things were slowing at the Columbia Restaurant and there really wasn't much more for me to do there. I wanted to continue in construction — you know, as a legitimate day job — and money wasn't coming in like it used to.

Since leaving the Columbia, I began to drift away from Casey. I found a job as a carpenter in Bradenton Beach and, at this time, they were building these condominiums in Bradenton and Sarasota, so the roof fell out just completely on top of us and there was no work. I was working for a company on Bradenton Beach and there was a whole group of us — a lot of hippies and bikers — because you don't get Joe Schmo with a nice suit on to come swing a hammer on the beach when it's 90 degrees outside, I can tell you that.

Danny Herb and his brother Clare ran the business, and they were bikers from Ohio. He had subcontracted this job from another guy out of Alabama. This guy is supposedly popping taxes out for us but we soon found out that wasn't true. One day we showed up for work and his construction trailer and all of his shit is gone. It was Friday and everybody wanted to get paid. There were like 20 or 30 of us, and Danny didn't have the money. He was a subcontractor and expected this guy to pay him.

Danny said that he'd pay us out of his own pocket when he could, but for the time being he suggested we all go down to unemployment and see what we could do. Well, you can't get unemployment if your employer doesn't pay into it. We found that out the hard way. The asshole screwed us all really bad, Danny included, and I had nothing else to do; I had no money. My mind went into overdrive mode again just trying to think of what I could do to make some bucks.

Janice knew some guys from Louisville who wanted to get Colombian marijuana, and Colombian marijuana was getting to be a big thing right then in the 70s — red bud, gold bud. If you're familiar with pot, you know how good that was, and everybody wanted it. Her friends asked if I could get any, and I didn't really know where to start.

Money drives my motivation for selling pot so I thought about all of my contacts. You'll remember my friend Lonnie back in Titusville was a beach bum and he smoked a lot of pot. I called him up and he said he wasn't doing that right now, but he had a friend in Gainesville named Steve Hullen who was a student down there. Lonnie said he'd just hook me up with him. I couldn't believe how good this was falling together because it was fast.

I was eating Walt's grouper sandwiches for dinner, lunch, everything. Old man Walt — he took really good care of me. He knew I was starving and he gave me the biggest grouper sandwiches I ever saw in my life, I'll never forget them. He helped me out a lot.

It doesn't sound like much, but when you don't have any money— I mean, these grouper sandwiches were hanging over the bun.

Janice and I are scraping dollars together, scraping nickels. We lived on 2nd Street in an old Sarasota home. I went to the Salvation Army and they gave us a $5 food card to spend. We bought chicken, a lot of chicken. All the while, I'm trying to put together some way to do a pot deal because I'm reverting back to my old drug dealing days in Detroit.

I finally meet up with Steve Hullen in Gainesville, and he tells me he can get me some red bud Colombian. It was like $285 a pound, but you had to buy 50 pounds.

My guys in Kentucky said they could swing that. I took a bus to Gainesville and I met these guys at a Holiday Inn, right by the first exit of Gainesville. It took every penny I had to get on that bus but I was determined to make this work.

I'm out exploring all over again; no more pill selling, still a pot smoker, and now I want to smuggle marijuana. I'm getting proactive now and thinking into the future. I'm going to smuggle marijuana. No more just selling it because I found out there was a huge demand and Florida was a hot spot. I wanted to get in with the right people, make the right connections, so I hooked up with Steve Hullen and did a 50-pound bale deal.

After the deal took place at the hotel, Hullen left. We've got this bale in the room and then two state troopers pull up right in front of our room. Naturally, we think, *oh shit, we're busted*, right?

Well, they were just checking in, but we've been smoking weed. Red bud Colombian has a strong odor. I mean, you can smell that half a mile away. It smells like hash burning. So we're a bit panicked and began stuffing towels under the doors in an attempt to block the smell.

We threw the bale in the bathtub and pulled the curtain shut because, in our reeling minds, that was the smartest thing to do. There's no other way out of the hotel but through our front door and past the troopers. We had no choice but to sit it out.

So that's what we did for 14 hours.

We had no room service, we quit smoking dope, and we just waited. We knew they weren't going to bust us by now because they had come with their hangers and moved them into their room. They weren't there for us but we stayed as low as possible.

Anyway, after a long night, the cops left. I split as fast as I could and ended up making $10 a pound, that was $500. Now $500 in the 70s when you're broke and eating chicken and grouper sandwiches and scraping nickels together is a lot of money. I went home with my chest out, feeling really good, really big about myself. Steve Riddle and his buddy Dilbert Butz contacted me and said they want to do this regularly. It didn't take me long to agree to it and I decided that I was going to work at that.

Anyway, time passes, nothing happens. One day they call me up because it's time and they want to do it again. Only this time they want 150 pounds. I get a hold of Steve Hullen. Steve says he can do it. Back to Gainesville we went and did it again. We did a bunch of them this way and it went on for a while.

As time went on, I earned a decent stash of money. I'm not getting along with my girlfriend of course, because now I'm acting like a big shot and drinking heavily again. Back to my old tricks, you see; money, alcohol; forget about other people. I was moving up the ladder and I was going to be a Colombian drug smuggler. This is what I decided. Here goes, it's going to happen for me. So I did another deal with these guys, and this one was, like, 250 pounds. Now you've got to understand, every time I'm making a dime a pound, that's $10. So 250 pounds, $2,500. 500 pounds, $5,000. I started to collect a good hit of some loot and it happened within 6 months.

I started going to a bar called Foley's Follies in downtown Sarasota. Things between Janice and I are not going well because my money went to my head. I forgot that she helped me get the connections. This is what happens when alcohol and greed come to play. You forget about the important things in life. At the moment I didn't care or even register how I treated her. I only cared about the money and finding fun. Well, I found a girl named Christine at Foley's Follies. Like I said, I have regrets when it comes to how things turned out with Janice.

The guys decided they wanted to get, like, another 500 pounds in one shot, and I got a hold of my friend Steve Hullen.

In the interim, I had taken a trip over to Daytona Beach and I met some guys who talked about doing a smuggle. Well, I had their phone numbers and I met a little guy named Frito, we called him Puentes, Little Wonder. Everybody had nicknames in this business. I gave Frito my telephone number, and told him that if he ever needed anybody to do anything, I'd do it. I didn't care because I knew there was money in it. He kind of shrugged it off, like, yeah, sure, blah, blah.

Anyway, a deal came up and these guys wanted 500 pounds. Steve Hullen told me he could get it, but we had to go to New Orleans. There was a load on a shrimp boat that came to Shreveport so we had to go there for the deal. I told Steve Riddle and Dilbert Butz to meet me in New Orleans. I planned to fly there from Sarasota, check into a hotel, and do our regular deal.

Well, we got to New Orleans and Steve Hullen met me there, and we just sat in the hotel. After a few days of just sitting and waiting,

Steve got a call. It turned out that the other guys were all out. Remember, I got two guys sitting there wanting to buy 500 pounds of pot, you understand, and I immediately see the dollar signs for me. This was going to be my good hit but now I have to find a way to get 500 pounds of weed. It was five Gs. That's a lot of money.

I had to tell my friends that I couldn't get it, and Steve Hullen had people from Cleveland, Ohio, and all over the country there to buy 500 pounds. There were a bunch of people sitting there with cash who couldn't get any pot. So I decided I was just going to go get drunk. Fuck it. I'm going to get drunk, that's my plan. I threw my hands up in the air because nobody could get the pot. Fuck it.

I head to the lobby and as I'm going out through the revolving doors, would you believe Frito "Puentes" was coming in through the other side. I just kept going around and followed him because, immediately, I knew that meant pot. I grabbed him by his shoulder and he turned around and recognized me. I said, "Man, I heard there was a lot of Colombian pot here. I've got a lot of people that want it but I can't get it." He said, "I can get you all you want."

Bingo. Now, if this isn't destiny, I don't know what is. What are the chances of me popping into this guy? Not great. We got to talking and set this thing up. Now, you've got to remember I only had two customers from Kentucky. Steve Hullen had customers from all over the country who were waiting to get it. I quickly became a guy who was going to sell 10,000 pounds of marijuana in trunk loads.

The way this all works is you have to put all the money up front, trucks are loaded with the pot, and then we all drive to a stash house. It was on a farm way out of town.

The night before this all went down, everyone was just waiting in the hotel room and talking. We had been smoking pot and now we're hungry. I ventured out into the Holiday Inn to see what I could find for food.

I found this little conveyor belt like they have in restaurants that brought the dishes around and then they go through this little booth type structure that is on the conveyor belt. Well, I crawled through that in the middle of the night and found myself in the main kitchen.

I spotted a huge refrigerator and I went straight for it. I found the biggest bowl of genuine crab salad you ever saw in your life.

I snatched that up, crawled back through the little booth thing, and showed up in the room.

There were a lot of people who I didn't know before this night and now I'm sharing a massive bowl of crab salad with them. We munched on that all night long just waiting to do the deal. From that night, my nickname became 'Crabby'. We had Little Wonder, Tito, Crabby, Puentes, the Dirtball, the Glove, everybody had nicknames. The next day, things went just as I planned. We loaded trunks and I walked away with $10,000.

Frito, Tito, and Nina (the wife of another partner of mine) had done this one smuggle, some thousands of pounds in Falmouth, Massachusetts. We had to sit in a hotel in Falmouth and wait for a boat to come into harbor. We were transporting marijuana back and forth, and the boat's code name was Yellow Submarine. It was, like, a 13,000-pound boat. Twelve-thousand pounds of pot on it is what I'm saying. We had a decent cut in the action, and it was quite a nice haul.

This one particular day, I pulled in around $60,000-$70,000. It was time to celebrate, right? I wanted to party a little with Frito, and he had rented this little car — I think it was a Hyundai, but they were real new back then. It was tiny and not very sturdy.

So we're driving through the mountains in New York, and we had already been partying so we're not thinking straight. Frito wasn't paying attention and we blew right through a stop sign. By the time I looked to my right, there was a pick-up truck right on us. He was probably going, like, 75 miles an hour. He T-boned us and we flipped over. My dog Charlie was with us too, sitting in the backseat.

We bounced, rolled, bam, boom, and landed upside down, teetering by a guardrail. I remember immediately smelling gasoline. I had smashed into Frito, and Charlie was still in the backseat. I think Charlie got knocked out, and I know I was dazed because I had hit my head on the rearview mirror. I reached over and shook Frito, tried to wake him, but he was knocked out. I felt a pain over my eye and reached and felt a cut over my eyebrow. My side also hurt real bad because the truck slammed right into the passenger side. Frito finally came to, and I helped him out of the car. Then I pulled Charlie out of the car who was awake now but he was acting funny. I think he was in shock.

The car is on its side, on a guardrail separating the road from the side of the mountain. Down below is death. I got everybody away from the car, and we laid down against some rocks. Then the ambulance sirens sounded in the distance and grew louder. It felt like it took hours for them to get there, but I know it was only minutes. Somehow, the people in the pick-up truck were hurt worse than us, which is a surprise since we were in this tiny little car.

I could still smell gasoline. The only sense that worked was my sense of smell, and it was working good. They sprayed foam on the gasoline to neutralize it. The ambulance and EMTs sped up and rushed to assess the situation. They both said they didn't expect to see anyone survive this crash; they expected fatalities and I distinctly remember one of them saying, "God was watching out for you tonight."

They were right, we should've been dead. Thanks God.

Don't even think God's not watching your ass, because He is. This is a Godly book. Am I a Jesus freak or a Godaholic? Yeah, I guess I am. Let's get that straight right now. And there were several times that I should've been dead.

Since Frito was a fugitive at the time, he wouldn't talk to the EMTs. They thought he was just out cold. He had phony IDs so there wouldn't be an issue. We were admitted to a hospital in New York where they gave me all kinds of X-rays and tests. Everything miraculously turned out okay for me.

You know, I was just starting to see the signs of the negativity from the life I lived, but I hadn't caught on yet. I was watching friends die from alcohol and drug abuse, and I believe these people became guardian angels. I was starting to believe that they watched over me because, I mean, there's no way all of my near-death misses were coincidences. No way it was luck.

I met this guy from Cleveland, Ohio, named Craig. He came through Steve Hullen, but now he's a new connection. In one night, I pulled 10 Gs, met smugglers, outlets across the U.S., and I'm feeling great. I'm really thinking I'm a cool guy. I've got money, I've got Christine, a really beautiful woman who I had met at Foley's — as far as I'm concerned my shit doesn't stink, to be honest with you. I dumped one of the sweetest girls in the whole world and I just met another beautiful one. I thought God was on my side. Little did I know the plans He had for my ass later on in life.

I'm doing a lot of deals now, things are stepping up. I'm getting marijuana for Hullen's friends from my friends in Daytona Beach. I'm getting pot for Kentucky. I've also made a pretty good deal with some Cleveland people, and I've had contact out of St. Louis. Not to mention the Pottsey Boys out of Madison, Wisconsin. We've got all these connections across the nation. This is a big deal for us.

I moved to Kentucky and stayed at a farm in a small town called Brownsville, about an hour and a half southwest of Louisville. I moved into Steve Riddle's stash house with him and his wife, Pat. She really wasn't his wife, more of his old lady, I guess. Steve had really long hair, a bald head, and a weathered face that resembled Gabby Hayes. In fact, that's why his nickname was 'Gabby Hayes'. Gabby's old lady, Pat, was pretty rough around the edges. She liked to shoot guns, smoke cigarettes, and every other thing out of her mouth was "you motherfuckers." She was our own version of Annie Oakley.

We drank a lot — and I mean a lot — on the farm. Steve and Pat lived on the edge and liked to pair alcohol with quaaludes. I liked alcohol and anything. I didn't care what it was, neither did they. In this private life we led, we just hung out and did drugs together. We stayed secluded at our stash houses. Making friends wasn't a concern of ours because we liked the solitude and anonymity at the farm.

Steve was a wife beater. I mean, this guy beat the shit out of his girl like there was no tomorrow. Like other times when I watched my buddies beat their wives or girlfriends, I never got in the way of it. If you remember, I was used to violence and actually thought being punched was normal. I didn't think a whole lot of the fact that he beat his old lady. I didn't like it, but I stayed out of it. He hit her for no damn reason. If he said, "Pat, get me some ice cream," she'd jump right up and get it for him from the kitchen. When she brought it back, he'd slap it out of her hand and just start punching on her. This guy was sick. All the Quaaludes, snorting coke, drinking rum, whiskey, whatever; listening to rock and roll, none of it helped the situation. I didn't do anything to stop it, which makes me feel like I played a role in the abuse Pat received.

But, you know what, money and smuggling was everything to me at the time, so I didn't say anything. I'd break up the fight and just tell Steve to take it easy. Pat never left. She just took it and walked around that place with a fat lip, a black eye, or a bruise somewhere. That was the fucked up lifestyle of that guy.

I told my friends about Steve and how he treated Pat. They thought he was a sick fuck. You know what, he was a sick fuck. I really hope he got his shit together. I know Pat died and Steve has kids, so I pray he has changed his ways.

Even though I was living at the stash house with Steve and Pat, I sold marijuana all across the United States, load after load. I was making serious money. I had hundreds of thousands of dollars laying around, just like you'd go into your closet, I could go pull out $50,000 or $100,000 without batting an eye.

People all over the country would call me about a shipment. There's pot in Louisiana; South Carolina; a boat just came in; go here, go there. I would then call other people in Cleveland, New York, Tallahassee, all over the country and have them check into hotels. There was a never ending stream of Colombian marijuana. I was right in the thick of it.

I cut my hair off and wore nice, regular-folk clothes to check into hotel rooms. I needed to blend in at hotels. Everybody was there waiting for a load that was coming.

The Cubans started doing freighters full of pot. The grade of marijuana was really going down, it was becoming commercialized. You could still get red bud and gold bud — everyone wanted that — but you couldn't get it in these big shipments. The Cubans didn't give a shit what they put on those freighters. Don't get me wrong, there was some good pot in there, but you didn't get to sit around and pick it out. It's not like going to Eddie Bauer and searching through stacks of the same shirt for the right size and color. You got 500 pounds of whatever was given to you and then you loaded trucks.

That worked. It's what we called "commercial".

Of course we wanted the gold and red bud. Hell, we were all pot smokers and wanted the Real McCoy. Who wouldn't? We were self-medicating with marijuana and actually acted and felt better with straight pot than we did when we were on a combination of cocaine, marijuana, alcohol, and Quaaludes. You don't act too bright when you're doing all that, believe me. And you become a pompous asshole when you're making a lot of money like we were.

Every last one of us thought we were hot shit, buying nice cars, being cool. We lifted ourselves up so high that someone really needed to have pulled the pedestal right out from under us, to be honest with you.

Anyway, that went on for quite a while…smuggling. I wanted to smuggle. I enjoyed the thrill, the position it put me in. Once I started in the business and got a taste of that life, my sights were set on becoming a Colombian marijuana smuggler. I didn't want to smuggle any other kind of pot, I wanted to smuggle Colombian red and gold bud and nothing else. In order to do that, to have a whole load of gold and red, you had to pick it out.

Remember Frito? My buddy who we called "Fuentes," the Little Wonder, who I met at what I call the Revolving Door? Well, I started talking more and more to Frito about getting in on other deals. My buddies, Denny Potts, The Glove, and DB a.k.a. Dirt Ball are all in Daytona and we're all a bunch of smugglers, right. I was moving a ton of pot around the country for these guys and we had a pretty solid relationship.

These guys decide they're going to do a smuggle on a DC4 aircraft. This plane will hold about 14,000 pounds of cargo so the potential profit is really high. They had an ex-Eastern Airline pilot who they called Tall Man and another pilot called Cowboy who had both turned to smuggling. They could make half a million bucks smuggling a load of marijuana in just a day so there was no need to fly commercial anymore.

Anyway, Tall Man happened to be a major alcoholic, too. He liked making a whole bunch of money, getting drunk, and not having to worry about being an Eastern pilot any more. That pretty much sums up Tall Man. He didn't smoke pot, but he should have.

I knew these guys were getting ready to do a DC4 job, and since I had friends all over the country, I was gold to these guys. I was a well-connected middle man. They needed outlets because they wanted to be paid cash. Not everyone can pay for 500 pounds up front when you're talking $250-300 a pound. I mean, we're talking $125,000-$150,000 up front, and I knew guys who could get us that cash. They needed me and I knew it. And I needed them.

Leading up to the week of New Year's, I got a phone call while a friend of mine and I were down in the Keys. We were just sitting tight, waiting. We didn't go out to party because we knew this deal was about to go down and we needed to be ready. Besides, we didn't mind missing out on the parties because once the job was done, we were going to party again. I'm not talking a little partying where we get high and just hang out. I'm talking whores, bags of coke, liquor, everything.

Now I know it's pretty disgusting for your average person to watch but it was part of our lifestyle. Like I've always said, a lot of these guys were very, very nice guys deep down.

I think all human beings are pretty nice, actually. We just get corrupted and demented, and money is dirty shit. I hate to be the one to break it to you, especially if you're in the grind right now just trying to make big bucks. No matter how you get it — the money — it can cloud your judgment. With the right intentions, it can do really good things, but when you're living outside the law, you're kind of abandoned. You're an outlaw, so you spend your money in outlaw ways.

Anyway, these guys made it and I got the phone call to come and get it in South Carolina. Now, as I'm told, the DC4 ran out of gas and had to land. When they took off in Colombia, DB was riding in the back. The load shifted and he almost got crushed by 14,000 pounds of marijuana. But he made it. They made it. They landed the plane and deserted it, but not before unloading all the pot.

They did it.

They got away with flying 14,000 pounds of Colombian marijuana and landed somewhat safely. I don't think Tall Man ever did another smuggle after that because he wanted $1M for that deal. Later in life, he was found dead in a bathroom at some beach house in Daytona Beach. Another one bites the dust, as I say. The end product for most everybody in this line of work isn't very promising.

Once again, the money and thrill was going straight to my head. I wanted to put together my own smuggles. My buddies and I got together and we planned it out. Frito and his partner, Tito, an Iranian guy, and Tito's girlfriend, a Russian named Nina, were all in on it. Nina — a beautiful girl — hauled money around. Frito and Tito were partners and they had hooked up with Lee and Les from the Carolinas.

Les and Lee had a really, really good thing going. We started making a lot of money off their smuggling on Morgan sailboats in Massachusetts. When we knew the boats were hauling a load, we would put up $50,000 as an investment. When all was finished, it was possible to get four times that investment plus a couple thousand pounds of that marijuana to sell. After you sell that marijuana at a wholesale price, we're talking about $300,000 to $400,000. That's some big money, my friend, no matter who the fuck you are.

We did this deal for a while and everybody's stacks were growing taller and taller. I made some big money during those investment days. I don't know if I can say this for tax purposes but, hell, at one point I had $1.2M buried in my mother's backyard in Florida. At 22 years old, I was stashing my cash, drinking, partying—acting like a big shot pot smuggler.

That self-important attitude crept into my mindset and I wondered why we were financing other smugglers when we could just finance our own for a greater profit. My friend Denny and I decided to do a DC3 job. So we bought a DC3. Guess who gets elected to go to Colombia to pick out weed?

Yours truly. You better believe I was game. It was my job to go pick it out in exchange for a thousand pounds of weed to sell and an extra fifty grand. Hell yes, I took it.

Well, Denny, DB, and I are supposed to meet some other guy named Nicky because he had supposedly paid off a cop who was going to secure a landing strip. This is in '77 going into '78. He's got this cop in Alabama and I'm in Georgia staying in this apartment. Nicky and I have to get to Alabama.

When we get to Alabama, we check into a hotel room and these two guys show up. They don't look like pot smokers and definitely not smugglers. Actually, they look like cops, but DB and Denny wanted to do this deal here.

As soon as I met these guys, I felt a sense of dread. Something wasn't right. I just had a really bad feeling about these two guys. We talked about the job and they said they'd be back in a few hours. We all agreed on that and I acted cool with them.

As soon as they left, I told Nicky that we were getting the fuck out of there. He asked where we were going and I said, "The fuck out of here. There's something bad about to go down here."

And, boy, thank God my instincts took over.

We flew back to Georgia and I immediately went to the apartment and I stripped what I could of my own to get it out of there.

Then I split.

Nicky went back to St. Louis and I got a hold of my buddies by pay phone and told them not to do the DC3 job. I explained that I believed those guys to be undercover cops, and not to load or send the plane. They all thought things were fine and they would move forward as planned. I tried to talk them out of it. I said, "Don't send the plane, don't load it. Something is wrong!" Well, they did it and they got busted.

Turns out this sheriff I met was Sheriff 'Big Jim' Clark. Now, 'Big Jim' Clark, for some of you who may be too young to know, was the police chief in Selma, Alabama who abused his power and beat Black protestors with his nightstick, and was known to advocate the use of cattle prods. He was a complete racist asshole. He reeked of bad energy and I felt it when we met in Alabama at that hotel.

My instincts were spot on and that is something that has helped me get out of a lot of bad situations. He ended up getting popped for it.

Anyway, we got away and they never snitched on me because that cop — 'Big Jim' Clark — didn't know my name, nobody knew who I was. The feds eventually ended up going to the apartment in Aceworth, Georgia because records show that I lived there.

But when the DEA went there for me, I was nowhere to be found. Plus, they couldn't connect me to the case. Take that as a lesson for you: if you feel something deep enough you better go with it, trust your gut. My buddies had to go to prison because they didn't trust me or my instincts.

Do you think for one second that scared me out of this business? Hell no. I carried on with Frito and Tito. We decided we were going to keep moving with the sailboats idea. It was something that worked well in the past so let's just keep that up. We all know by now that I got money on the brain and that took over yet again. I thought we should do our own plane deal, and this time I wanted a DC6. You know, a DC6 is a very large airplane that can hold 26,000 pounds of cargo. From selling 50-pound bales to chartering a DC6, I considered myself successful at this point.

But before we move into that job, we need to finish the boats we're currently working. Frito sends me to Colombia to pick out the product. He's in the United States still, but he had some phone numbers to connect me with people in Colombia. He remained in the background, but I had told everybody I'd do whatever I had to do, I want to be up all the way in this one.

I flew to Barranquilla, the largest city in the northern Caribbean Coast region of Colombia and walked straight through customs. They didn't make me do anything, they just let me go through where the Colombians were waiting for me. Customs was obviously paid off. I scooted right around; they knew who I was and called me over. We got into a BMW and drove away.

A short drive later and I'm at a little landing strip where I board a private plane with a Guajiro Indian named Chachichu. He was a heavy set guy and big — body guard BIG.

We flew to this town in the middle of nowhere. It turned out to be San Juan, Colombia, and we went to a tiny village where chickens and pigs are just roaming free. There are guys with straw hats and no teeth, little kids playing in the streets. Chachichu took me to his wife's house where I stayed during this trip. When I got there, they brought me rubber sandals — the kind you can get at the dollar store — and Marlboros and Coca-Cola.

I really didn't speak any Spanish so I had to use a little translation book I had picked up back home. They locals would say, "Marlboro", "Coca-Cola"? I'd reply, "Yeah, bueno, bueno."

They were very nice to me and, despite being very poor, they were quite generous. Homemade dishes, sandals and a towel, cigarettes, and Coke to drink — I'm sure it was a lot for them to do for me, and I appreciated everything. They wanted me to feel at home. After I had a shower – usually a long one because the water just dripped and dripped – I walked out and they would say, *"Mr. Jerry, Coca-Cola? Marlboro?"*

I'd say, *"Yeah, si. Bueno!"*

One day I noticed a young girl peeking through the windows, probably 16 or 17. She was giving me 'the eye' — you know what I'm talking about — because I was a gringo. The locals wanted to marry Americans, okay. It was a lifeline for many of them. She would place little matchboxes on my windowsill and tell me she loved me.

Yeah, right, I'm going to be the special guest at the town's next shotgun wedding if I touch this girl. She was absolutely ugly in the face, but what a beautiful body. I was tempted, I admit. I'm no Goody Two-Shoes, remember. Anyway, nothing happened. I ended up getting really tight with them.

They took me way up in the mountains to pick out the weed because that's where they stashed it. I jumped in the back of a pickup truck with a bunch of Colombians. We all crowded together, they put a straw hat on me, and we had little blankets and shit around us. It was a pretty quiet ride as we took rural routes up toward the mountains.

We went through a few checkpoints, but it was obvious to me that they were paid off because we were just waved right on through.

As we drove deeper into the mountains, I began noticing men in trees.

Armed men in trees.

I knew we must be getting close to the destination. After a long drive, we finally pulled up to this little shack where a guy sat lookout in front on a little—like— shitty lounge chair.

At first glance he looked like a typical Colombian with a hat, very average clothes, but then on second glance I saw the gun belt he wore slung across his chest. You know, the kind you see in a Mexican gun fight movie. He's got a rusty pistol stuffed in his pants, and a rifle. Behind him, the shack was about the size of three outhouses put together. This is where they stashed the red bud and gold bud.

A couple guys went with me as I walked inside. I was worried that the house — if that's what you could call it — was going to topple right on my head. So I picked through the stash and selected the load of pot that I wanted. The Colombians were going to put it on a boat in Marlboro cartons. In fact, I would recognize the cartons because you marked them with a magic marker making it easy to spot. Each farmer had his own mark for his particular crop.

And right then, standing out in the middle of nowhere, on top of a pretty tall mountain in Colombia, one of these guys offers me a cold Heineken! I rolled a big splif, had a cold Heinie, looked out over the Colombian mountains and thought *it doesn't get much fucking better than this.*

We headed back down the mountain and, before we went back to where I was staying, we stopped at the local bar for some *cerveza.*

We talked as best we could given my broken Spanish and their broken English but it was a good time. They wanted me to send back T-shirts and cowboy boots, okay, *zapatos.* And they liked my sunglasses because the one guy that was at the stash house was infatuated with them. They were Foster Grants with the transition lenses that would lighten when you were inside and darken in the bright sunlight. He loved them so I was going to find some to send back on the boat for him.

I became really friendly with a lot of these locals, and I wasn't afraid of them because they turned out to be very humble people, actually. They just saw me as a gringo who could bring their village money that they desperately needed. They were not really criminals, these people. They were very nice.

Plus, they let me watch a lot of "Kojak". It was in Spanish but, what the hell? I didn't care. I had "Kojak", Marlboros, and Coca-Cola.

Boy, was I happy.

CHAPTER FOUR

Desperado

After I left San Juan, I flew to fucking nowhere-land where we could use payphones at another little village. I called Frito to let him know that I picked out the load and things were a go. He was going to then pay them a downstroke of $40,000 on the weed. The cost of the weed to us was $10 a pound!

The two Colombians who were with me were a couple of thugs. They weren't the laborers that I had been staying with in San Juan. They would have been scary looking to normal people but, you know, I was mental so it didn't scare me at all. They wore decent clothes and always had a pistol tucked in their waistband.

After I called Frito, we drove to Barranquilla. It was vastly different than the tiny village I had just spent time in. I'm getting excited about the prospect of this big job and the shitload of money I was about to make.

We stopped for some food and while we were there, word got to the guys I was with that the money never came through. Frito was supposed to have paid it in Miami but, for some reason, it never came through.

You know who they were looking at?

Yep, yours truly.

Suddenly I became a piece of material to them, a pawn.

Ransom.

They weren't going to release any of the pot I had just selected, and they began getting nervous that I might be a cop or something. Somebody fucking screwed up because I'm all alone out here and all I've got is a little book of Spanish phrases to get me through this mess.

That's not going to save my life.

My "escorts" took me to this little part of Barranquilla that wasn't the nicest part of town. It wasn't the worst part of town either.

They secured my wrists with zip ties and brought me to a pretty decent apartment. They were able to get across to me that I wasn't going anywhere until things were straightened out. They knew things weren't right, I knew things weren't right, and it was a pretty stressful situation. Eventually, they brought in a friend named Ramone. He was able to interpret for them and that's when I learned that they hadn't received the money. I thought, *oh, fuck*. Somebody better pay because, if not, I won't be coming back to the United States any time soon.

Or ever. I'll end up dead in the jungle.

For a couple weeks I was in this apartment. They brought me food, 18-year-old prostitutes, Johnny Walker Red, little bags of pretty pink— it was good cocaine, actually—and bags of pot. I could pretty much do anything I wanted *except leave the apartment.*

The thugs were there and snorted coke, drank, and smoked cigarettes one after another. They never let the pistols out of their waistbands, which would tend to make you nervous. Now…I'm only 23 years old, all alone, praying for someone back home to do something quick…*fucking* quick.

Finally, the phone rang and they just stared at me. This was the call that would determine my fate. Am I going home, or am I going to some six-foot hole in some remote part of the jungle?

One of them picked up the phone and, of course, the conversation was all in Spanish so I couldn't follow. He hung up and gestured for me to get dressed. We were leaving but I still didn't know where we were actually going. I didn't know if I was going to hell or heaven, or if I was going to be set free.

They marched me out the door toward a little BMW. The cartel had a lot of little BMWs these guys rode around in.

We drove closer to the coastline and up to a huge house with a significant amount of property surrounding it. Guys were walking around the place with rifles strapped on their backs. A rough-looking older guy in his 40s was waiting for us as we entered this beautiful house.

The interpreter that was with me in the apartment is still around. He put his arm around me and he said, "You know they like you. Because if they didn't like you..." He slid his finger across his throat.

"Don't be scared. You're okay."

Scared? Who...me?

One day, Miro Mendosa, who was the head Mafioso in his particular faction, and I are standing in the living room looking out of the front window admiring the scenery when a car pulls up. A couple Cubans get out of the car and Miro's guys meet them at the car. An argument breaks out and Miro's men pull pistols and *pop, pop, pop.* The Cubans crumble to the ground.

Dead. Just like that.

I'm trying not to spill the cup of cafe con leche I'm holding when two Federale cars pull up, load the dead guys in the trunk, and drive off. Another guy comes out and cleans the driveway with some shit, and Miro continues sipping his coffee like nothing happened. Nerves of steel, this guy.

I eventually found out that these Cubans had told the Colombians that something happened with their cocaine deal, and Miro found out they were lying. That was the price to pay, and I'm pretty sure it was set up at that time to send me a message as well. Message received loud and clear: don't fuck around.

I stayed surprisingly relaxed when Miro's buddies came back inside, even though I probably had to change my fucking shorts later. I'd never seen anybody get popped before.

Time carries on here and I eventually meet Rene Benitez, another business acquaintance of Miro's. Frito's plan is to meet me at a place called the Don Blas in Cartagena. Benitez gave me the creeps; he made my skin crawl. While I knew him, he scared the shit out of me, but he also took good care of me. Of course, I had to act like I liked him.

Benitez and his men walked around Cartagena with their chests out, like it was the fucking wild west. No shit. They carried pistols in their front pockets, in the waistband of their pants tucked in like a posse of wannabe cowboys. The Federales, the coppers, everybody knew them and patted them on their backs all over Cartagena. I have no idea how much money or "perks" he slipped the cops, but it was obvious he was doing it because he could do anything he wanted. I don't know, but I do know that I didn't like that guy one bit. Years later, I was in Sarasota on parole and I saw his picture hanging in the post office as one of the FBI's "most wanted."

I hung around with him for a while until Frito could straighten things out for our DC-6 deal. A couple other heavy duty gangsters came marching around the Don Blas a lot. I mean, all the cocaine cowboys were in and out of Cartagena and Cali.

These guys weren't built up like everybody thinks, they're spooky. Hollywood glamorizes these guys and makes them out to be very clean, well-dressed, smooth talkers. I'm here to tell you that these dudes were nothing like that. Their shirts were hanging half out. They were sloppy pissers, and always had a drip on the front of their pants. They snorted cocaine and had shit in their noses all the time. I mean they were pigs. And they scared the shit out of me, too.

I tried to act as normal as I could because what are you really going to do? When in Rome, right? I just joined in and pretended like I liked them, but I wanted to get the fuck out of there!

Finally, the day comes that I find out I'm going home. They kept me around to make sure the money was really coming through and, when it did, Frito showed up to take me home. We went back to Daytona Beach and hung around for a while and kept on smuggling.

When I got home, I purchased some Rottweilers because I had been thinking about raising dogs and now I had money. My rotties— Cleveland, Kentucky, St. Louis, and Smuggles — were a fun way to take my mind off the business for a while each day. I was making a ton of loot, though, and I wanted more. Naturally. That's when we decided to start meeting about doing the DC-6. This is when the trouble began.

Frito was charged with finding a source for the plane we needed to purchase. He found a place out in Arizona which was like a graveyard for planes. I went out to Tucson so I could sneak around at night to look at the planes until I could find one. But I don't know anything about planes so how would I know if this one looks good or that one is too much work?

The Tucson connection showed me around the planes but, actually, I didn't think I could trust him. And, in fact, that turned out to be a dead end—a waste of time and money.

Frito hooked me up with an airplane broker named Jerry Lee Harvey, who became a well-known smuggler. I didn't know him at the time. We found a DC-6 for $350,000 that needed a little work done on it. It was over in Nicaragua, which was not ideal, but it would hold ten tons of marijuana, easy. Ten fucking tons meant this deal's going to take quite a bit of bread up front.

I had to get the money together to buy the airplane. Frito was in charge of getting the down payment for the marijuana. We came up with $500,000 and nothing was happening. Frito gave it to Lee Harvey. He had the money for quite a while and we all kind of wondered what's going on. Are we getting a plane or what? I had the pilots ready, but you can't just put a pilot in a plane. They need to practice with that plane for a while, know what they're flying. There's a lot of planning in these jobs. Moving parts, time, back and forth. It doesn't happen overnight. Frito found a landing strip in Charleston, West Virginia, so we had our plane, pilots, and landing location. We needed the cargo and Lee Harvey had our money still.

We decide we're going to get our money back. We're not going to do this job, so let's just get our money back.

Tito and Frito had rented this really fancy house in Boca, which we later found out belonged to Felix Williams, the CEO for Monsanto.

It was a big shot house in a gated community—pretty nice place.

My business partner from Cleveland, Craig, was with me, so we decided we'd just go to Tito and Frito and pick up the money. They had a friend hanging around with them, Pati. He was a French guy and pretty much just their gopher. We had met a few times prior and I didn't get a great vibe from him. Fact is, I didn't like him at all.

We went over for dinner and Tito's old lady was making a huge pot of lamb stew. After they gave us the strong box of cash, Tito said the stew was ready to eat. So we set our things, including the strong box, on the couch and went to the kitchen to eat. We realized Pati never came to the kitchen, but didn't really think anything of it.

We enjoyed our stew and we're just hanging out together. I'm feeling a little better now that we have the money. I know our plans for the DC-6 are on hold right now, but I know I'll find another way to get it going again. When we finished dinner, we went back to the living room. The strong box that was left on the couch was gone.

Long gone.

And so was Pati.

That fucker took off with the money!

Total panic sets in. Tito calls the front gate to tell them to stop any cars going out, but it was too late. Pati was long gone. You know when you lose half a million bucks in one crack, that's serious fucking money, which means serious fucking panic.

I know I talk about God and everything now, but I wanted to kill this guy. I never liked him to begin with and I sure didn't like him now.

I went into a complete and total freak-out because nobody really knew what move to make next. Tito said he'd probably go back to New York. Tito wasn't being much help and I kind of got a bad feeling about that. He didn't seem as upset about losing half a million like I was, and he wasn't offering too many options or suggestions. Other friends were invested in this job, and I was determined to get that money back.

We knew the guy's name — Pati Alterman — and we knew he was going back to New York, so we went to New York.

We called around to hotels and asked for patrons with the last name 'Alterman', and eventually we found him at the Helmsley Hotel.

They had a guest named Pati Alterman.

Bingo. We load up with pistols and knives, head to the hotel, and bang on the door.

Someone called, "Who is it?" from inside the room and I called back, "Room service," just like in the fucking movies.

Years later, a friend of mine, Matty, who worked for them, told me it was all a setup. Tito, Pati, Tito's girlfriend — they were all in on it. So I guess I never had a chance to find that money.

They opened the door. *Boom.* We went charging in there and pushed people up against walls. We were yelling at them, *"Where's the money?"*, *"Where's Pati?"*, *"Get the fucking money!"* I mean, we scared the shit out of these people.

Guess what. Wrong room.

These poor people — I don't mean to laugh — but I'm sure these poor people were scared to death. We were feeling pretty bad because not only is the deal called off, but we lost a lot of money.

We needed to regroup, so back to our old process we went. Invest, load boats, make some money. Repeat. Invest, load boats, make some money. We had to be strategic about what jobs we took and which ones we didn't. We needed people in certain places, to make arrangements to meet this guy here and get the money there. I mean, there's a lot of legwork involved in putting together a 20,000-pound load of marijuana to bring back to the United States.

Anyway, down payments are made again and we get a DC-6. Sky, the pilot we hired, came to us through Nicky. Frito was in Colombia picking out the bales, and he had to get it from different farmers and different groups so it wasn't quick work. Not everybody's just got 26,000 pounds sitting in their backyard.

We had to have some work done on the plane before the big day, so we moved it from Nicaragua to Miami. My girlfriend at the time, Christine, was a PanAm airline stewardess and she had an apartment right across from the Miami airport in Miami Springs. Christine let me use her apartment for a lot of meetings—like money transfers—because we're moving money around all the time now. You understand, you've got to pay for things to get fixed on the plane, and parts for a DC-6 are very expensive. Hell, fuel is a small fortune in itself. I mean, we're talking about a big ass airplane.

Now, when we get back to Sarasota, I started meeting with a pilot named Breck Dana Anderson, alias Jessie. Anderson has been caught before. He got busted in Morocco and ended up staying a couple years in a Moroccan jail. He was a hard guy, I'll say that, and he wasn't a snitch.

My job was to keep Sky and Anderson, our pilots, on ice and make sure they had food, money, whatever they needed. The longer people sit around, the more they start to have second thoughts because they're wondering, *Is this really going to come together? Do I really want to do this?* But when you're telling them they're going to get a quarter million dollars, and Sky was going to get half a million, that's not bad at all for one day's work. The lure of easy money is hard to pass up.

Sky wanted to back out, on and off, but I talked to him and he insisted that I be on that plane when we land in Colombia. He didn't realize I had no choice but to be on that plane because that piece of shit Rene Benitez was the loader and he already knew me. Benitez had to see a gringo's face that he knew. If these pilots just landed there by themselves, well…they probably wouldn't be flying away, let me put it that way.

Benitez and all those Colombians and Cubans just wanted to put cocaine on the planes and the boats. I always insisted that was not a good idea and said it was bad karma. Well, when I said "bad karma" to those people, they looked at me like I was some kind of mental case. They didn't know what that meant. When you think about it, I was fueling that negative energy because I was working with these guys, paying into it, so I really wasn't Mr. Good Guy. I financed a bunch of bullshit, still fed the animal.

There are no morals in this shit, let's get real. This is about money, okay? I thought I was high and mighty, making responsible choices by not letting the cocaine on the plane. What an asshole I was, thinking I was "clean." In reality, I was a criminal too. I was doing dirty business just like they were. I hate to say it, but I've got to take responsibility for it. All my friends—*all of us* —were criminals.

June 6, 1979 rolls around and all of our work over the past six months has paid off because we're ready. The pilots know where they're going, they've got all the coordinates, and West Virginia is expecting us. All systems are go. We have to fly from Lauderdale — we left at 5:00 in the morning — and a couple friends were there to see us off. They came to wave goodbye to us, I guess, and wish us good luck. I remember boarding the plane. It was dark as hell. We settle in and head to our first stop: Colombia.

After a six-plus hour flight, we landed on this long strip in the middle of nowhere and there were trucks waiting for us. They not only brought the marijuana, but fuel as well so we could have full tanks for our flight to West Virginia. There were four of us on board: Greg McCafferty; David Thomas Sesing, a.k.a. Sky; Brett Anderson; and me. Incidentally, McCafferty ended up pleading guilty to being a driver, but denied being on that plane. He beat that rap, in a sense, but Greg McCafferty was on the plane with us.

On the flight back, we had one engine that scared the shit out of me. It was believed to have been repaired but it backfired. Have you ever been in the air when an airplane engine backfires?

You'll shit your pants.

I had a bunch of those little bottles of liquor that you get on planes because my old lady was a Panam stewardess. Every time I heard that engine backfire, I drank another mini bottle of liquor. Between the engine and the fact that we had to dodge storms, I was pretty nervous for a while there. When we finally closed in on entering the United States again, we dropped low and we were just kind of right over the water.

I loved it.

I loved watching those big propellers churn that water in the moonlight, and I was thinking, *Fucking A, I'm smuggling marijuana into the United States.* I mean, it was a rush and I liked it. I really like it. I was hungry for it at that point in my life. I'm manic depressive, so I guess I was having a manic attack because I loved every minute of it.

As we approached Charleston, we gained a bit of altitude to wait to be cleared for our descent into Kanawha County Airport. We made our final approach at 1:00 in the morning. Sky and Anderson wanted to drop the landing gear to wash it off with the rain because they thought the dirt on the tires could be connected to Colombia.

I don't know what foolishness they were thinking, but they dropped the gear. Now, what everybody thinks happened is Sky and Anderson hit a switch and accidentally dumped our hydraulics because, when we touched down, we had no hydraulics.

They fought like hell to keep that plane straight. We were moving at a couple hundred miles an hour, we're hauling ass, and we have no hydraulics? The plane started to list to the right just as we touched down, and somehow, these pilots muscled the plane to at least partially straighten it out just after touchdown.

But now the runway was coming to an end. Suddenly that engine backfiring seemed like sissy stuff. I knew we were going to crash. The only words that anybody really said were, "Oh shit."

Smash, crash, boom.

I was in the middle engineer seat, McCafferty was behind me, and then the two pilots up front. Everything went flying. Some kind of radio gear broke loose and smacked me in the head knocking me out cold for who knows how long. It could've been 10 seconds, it could've been 10 minutes. I have no way of knowing. All I remember is when I came to, I was upside down in the cockpit. In fact, the whole plane was pretty much upside down, on the side of a mountain. All I could taste was the metallic twang of blood in my mouth, and I could feel it running down the side of my face. I was wearing a cross around my neck, and when I came to my senses, I realized I had it clutched in my fist.

I guess I thought it was the end of my life, the end of the road for me. I'm not sure what went through my mind during those moments. I'm sure I was protected by God, by my deeply hidden faith.

God saved me; saved all of us that day.

I climbed out of the cockpit and saw Sky coming up the side of the mountain. He was screaming, "Jessie, Jessie!"

I told him not to come up to the plane, Jessie's not in there. I'm not sure who Jessie was but that's the only person he was concerned about in the midst of the chaos. He yelled, "Jessie's going to die, Jessie's going to die!" I said, "Jessie's not in the plane." He must've been out of his wits.

I scrambled out of the front of the plane and couldn't catch my balance because not only were we on the side of the mountain, but I was dizzy from the knock on my head. Every time I stood up, I fell again. Plus, there are bales of marijuana rolling out from behind me, hitting me behind my legs, knocking me on my ass. I finally got enough balance to straighten myself up.

To my right, I saw Anderson. He was full of blood, his arm was bleeding really bad and his face looked like something out of a horror movie. He was hung up kind of upside down next to a tree.

David was climbing up the slope and McCafferty was at the bottom of the hill, crying. I had to get my wits about me. I knew I was probably the only one in the group who could think somewhat clearly.

I grabbed David who was still trying to go back up towards the plane. I said, "You can't do anything for anybody, and Anderson's over there." I pointed toward Anderson where he was out cold by the tree.

I said, "We've got to get the fuck out of here!"

This all happened fast and I realized that the engine is still running, the plane is still falling down the mountainside. A wing went about four or five feet over my head as it broke off from the main fuselage, and something was on fire in the cockpit.

An oxygen tank that was on the plane just exploded. Boom! Luckily we were all far enough away that we weren't hit by anything from the blast. In some ways, it was a beautiful sight. I hate to say it, but the gigantic flames were absolutely gorgeous.

I turned to David and said, "We've got to move, man," and David followed. McCafferty was already at the bottom where we were heading. We had no fucking idea where we were, so we started running down this little street, Keystone Lane.

So we're running down Keystone Lane and we start hearing sirens. Fire trucks, police cars; every time we'd see lights coming toward us in the distance, we would hide in the bushes along the side of the road. When the road was clear again, we were up and running again.

We don't know where in the hell we're going. We essentially just ran around in circles. One thing we didn't plan for was learning the layout of the airport and the surrounding area. We left that bit of planning out so it put us in a hard position to make good decisions.

We started noticing helicopters flying around the area after we were moving around for a couple hours, if I was gauging time correctly. I had to keep stopping because my head was split open, my mouth smashed in. My right leg was also fucked up so it was hard to walk, and I later learned I had busted ribs and had actually fractured my skull.

David was in pretty bad shape, too, because we learned that he had a punctured lung and wasn't breathing well. McCafferty wasn't hurt very bad so he lucked out. We left Anderson still hung up by a tree with half his arm ripped off and his face torn to pieces. None of us were in any shape to carry him and we desperately hoped he was okay.

Soon, we begin hearing dogs barking. It was like you see in the movies; cops with hound dogs chasing the perp.

Well, I was the perp, but these dogs weren't very good. They ran right past my feet as we were hiding in a bush. I heard the cops encouraging the dogs, "Good boy, good boy," and I wanted to jump up and tell them how that dog *ain't* no good, but I stayed put.

We found this little private aviation center and I gave McCafferty some change that I had tucked in my sock. He was in the best shape out of the three of us, so I told him to go up to the pay phone to call the house in Cleveland; tell them we're alive and in the woods. Then I told him to come straight back because the cops were going to be crawling all over this place. He said, "Okay, okay," and he ran up there.

He didn't go to the pay phone.

Instead, he went inside the building. From what I suspect, he went in and gave himself up because, within a matter of minutes, the cops pulled up and dragged him out of there. David and I watched it all go down. There goes McCafferty. Now it's just me and David.

My mind is reeling now. I'm trying to weigh our options; we could turn ourselves in or keep hiding and running until we find another pay phone. I'm scanning the area around us to look for a pay phone when I see one of the airplanes at this hangar we're near. I asked David, "How easy would it be to steal one of those planes, David, and just fly out of here?"

He said, "Oh, we can't do that, that would be air piracy."

I said, "David, we just dropped 26,000 pounds of marijuana on the side of the mountain there. Air piracy is not going to be that much of a bad charge for us 'cause we're already in a lot of trouble."

He didn't want to do it, which meant we kept wandering around. It was just as well we didn't try and steal the plane. David could not breathe any more as his lung filled with blood, and blood leaked out his nose. My forehead was split wide open and still bleeding badly.

We wandered around the area for about six or seven hours until the sun came up. We stopped at streams whenever we could so I could wash the blood out of my eyes, and then I'd lay down and let the blood coagulate. We'd get up and travel again. We didn't know where we were going…all we could do was hide.

David was tired, and his breathing was really ragged now, and he said, "Well, I'm giving up. I can't go any further and I can't breathe now." He had blood coming out his nose and he was spitting some up because he was bleeding from where his lung was punctured. I saw him walking down towards the highway and I said to myself, *I just can't let him go alone.*

I went to him and said I was coming with him. As soon as we get down to that highway, we're going to jail. We both knew it. I told David not to say anything when the cops show up. If they ask why we're bleeding so bad, we agreed we would just tell them that we got into a fight. I knew they wouldn't believe that but we were going to say it anyway.

Just as predicted, in a matter of a couple minutes there were more cops on us than you could imagine, guns pointed at us— pistols, rifles—they were acting like they caught Al Capone, way out in Charleston, West Virginia.

We were hauled off to the station and one of the cops said, "Boy, you fellas shouldn't even be walking around right now. Did you see the wreckage you left up on that hill?" We told him that we didn't know anything about anything on that hill. He didn't believe that bullshit for one second. They were pretty redneck-y, these cops.

The first thing they did was interrogate us—David in one room, me in the other. They already had McCafferty and I still believe he should've just done what I said in the first place, but I guess Destiny had a plan.

God was in charge of this.

After we went through the typical question/answer phase, they took us to the hospital and continued to ask questions. They said, "You know, if you give us some names, things will be easy, you can go home today."

Being the smartass I was I said, "Names? George Washington.

James Cagney. I don't know, what name do you want?" I wasn't going to talk. I was seasoned enough to know better, and David just kept his mouth shut.

At the hospital I was stitched up and cleaned up. The doctor who stitched me up made me look like Frankenstein. He said, "See what happens here when you bring drugs to West Virginia?" He was sending me a message thinking we were big drug dealers.

We were just a bunch of guys trying to smuggle a load of pot so we could retire happily ever after.

CHAPTER FIVE

Angels Fly Too Close to the Ground

After the events of the crash, I was arrested and taken into custody. I had a fractured skull, teeth were smashed, broken ribs, horrible bruises all over my torso — seriously bad shape.

As I said, I was briefly hospitalized in Charleston. Afterwards, we were bounced back bounced back and forth out of interrogation and then waiting in a holding cell. They'd question David while I waited, then get me and tell me that David had told them such and such. It was a tactic and I knew they were just trying to get us all to talk. We all kept our mouths shut.

I stayed in the Kanawha County Jail for quite a while. My bond was first set at, like, $1 million. I wasn't going anywhere with that bond, but I wanted to get David, Anderson, and McCafferty out of there. They were my responsibility because this was my plan, I was the lead on this smuggle. We couldn't find enough money to get all of us out so I made them my focus. I figured my sources on the outside would eventually help get me out. We just kept our mouths shut and stuck to the plan.

We had to go back and forth to the courthouse for hearings the whole time we were there.

You know, in Charleston at the time, it was a pretty big deal. Newspapers, reporters and cameras were on us. We were basically on the front page of the *Charleston Daily Mail* every single day. We kind of became celebrities.

As we go through all these hearings and this bullshit, lawyers are coming in from out of town. Jerrold Goldstein was a big shot from Texas; Keith Strope, who became the head of NORML; Ed Kagan, a Kentucky lawyer; Richard Chosid, my lawyer from Detroit; and a whole slew of lawyers from New York, Nick Esposito, Frank Sax, Allan Silver.

The prosecutors were Bob King, Tim DiPiero, Rebecca Betts, and Wayne Rich. These guys were hot shots. They're calling out motions and all kinds of stuff, and these other guys in Charleston, they didn't really know what the hell was going on. There was a degree of jealousy there from the arrogance of the hot shot lawyers. They were kind of beating up on these Charleston lawyers.

The county jail in 1979 Charleston, West Virginia was no picnic area. The bullpen – they didn't have any room for me in another part of the jail, so they put us in the mentally deranged part of the jail – was a nasty place. This was where the cuckoos were.

These guys, I'm telling you, they pissed on the floor. The place smelled like a sewer. The doors were electronic, so you had to go into your cell at night and bam, bam, bam, you'd hear the cell doors slamming shut. As you would imagine, the food wasn't very good either. It was a pretty bad scene. In fact, at that time, it was considered one of the worst county jails in the United States, which I learned after I got out of there. I had never seen anything like it and I'd already been to jail.

For a while, David and I had a cell together. I was on the bottom bunk and he was on the top. A jail cell is only so many feet wide and long, not very big. About enough space for the bunks, a toilet, and a couple guys to walk pace about 5 steps. In this part of the jail, there was a water pipe that ran across the ceiling through all the jail cells.

The night before a new inmate was brought into the cell next to ours. He was kind of making a fuss, a very strange character. The next day, we met him. His name was Howard Gershwin and, like I said, a goofy guy. They had picked him up at the airport wandering around, so they assumed he was involved with the marijuana plane crash. We all know that he had absolutely nothing to do with it. He was just a mental case, okay? Charleston police had brought him under suspicion.

Anyway, poor Howard — just a tiny, skinny guy — is scared to death with all these mugs and thugs. I mean, there were some dirty bastards in that jail, I'll tell you that right now. You weren't given a uniform or anything, just your street clothes, but they did take away your belt.

For some reason, they forgot to take away Howard's belt. Maybe it was because he wasn't under any kind of suicide watch or anything. I don't know what happened with that. This was just a couple days after Howard was brought in, and we're all laying around during the day. You had the option of closing your cell door and locking it, if you wanted.

So David and I are laying around in our cell, and most cell doors are open. Howard had locked himself in his cell. Nobody had scared him or anything, but we didn't think anything of it. I'm laying on my bunk and saw a ceiling pipe that runs through the cell wiggle. Then David and I both heard it clanking around and, just wiggling. David asked, "What in the hell is that."

I said, "I don't know man." I get up out of bed and we walk around. Howard's locked in his cell, hanging himself.

We're like... *shit.* We start screaming for the guards, but they don't come right away. We're watching this guy essentially committing suicide in front of us. He got himself strapped up and stepped off the bed, just dangling. Now everybody's screaming. Most are yelling for the guards to come help. Some guys, believe it or not, were yelling "do it!"

Finally, they threw the switch to open the doors and David and I ran into Howard's cell. David climbs up to get the belt off and I'm underneath him trying to hold him up to take the weight off so David can remove the belt. By this time, his eyes are bloodshot red and there's a trickle of blood running out of his ear. His coloring looked really bad.

David got the belt loose and we dragged him out of the cell. EMS got there just as we got him to the walkway and they went to work. Howard survived, thank God. His father was some big shot in the government somewhere and I heard through the grapevine that he called Judge Dennis Knapp, who was our judge at the time, and told the judge what we had done. I don't think that mattered to Knapp, but I thought it was nice of him to try. We saved Howard and that's a good thing. That's enough for me.

Another roommate, as I called them, was a guy named Jimmy Brown. He was a tall, skinny black guy who was bragging about this other guy that he had "fixed." Jimmy and his buddy were out for a joyride in his hot shot car with expensive aluminum wheels. He let his friend drive for a while and they hit a pothole, which flattened the rim, I guess. Jimmy Brown was telling the story and then, nonchalantly, said, "Yeah, so I got out of the car and I shot that motherfucker."

He killed the guy for messing up the rim on a car. That's what he was in jail for.

We had this other little short guy next to us and I'm kind of street savvy, but this was a new experience for me. Remember, this was the area of Charleston's jail where guys with mental issues were held. Needless to say, we had some cuckoos. This other guy — a little short West Virginian guy — wore a newsboy-style hat. You know, like Brian Johnson from AC/DC wore. We'd be laying around at night and you'd talk through the jail cell doors, through the bars. Everybody talked openly about their cases. Naturally, everybody said, "I'm innocent" or "they got the wrong motherfucker".

This little guy always made me laugh because he always said the cops got the right guy. He was guilty and he had no qualms about what he had done. He caught his wife in bed with his best friend, and he shot his wife in the head and then shot his best friend in the nuts. They both died. He would say, "Now I hear all you motherfuckers in here saying you're innocent, but I want everybody to know that they got the right guy."

This makes you laugh when you're in jail, I hate to tell you. This guy only got five years for this because he pleaded guilty to a crime of passion. In West Virginia, a crime of passion only got him five years for killing two people. Here I am looking at a lot of time for smuggling pot, okay?

It made no sense to me.

Eventually, my friends from Cleveland were able to spring me from jail and pay my bond. Finally, I heard my name called and they said, "You're out." I jumped off my bed so fast, got dressed, and there was a bondsman there named Surry. He was from Cleveland, Ohio. He was wearing a black leather jacket, big dude. He told me that my friends paid him to come get me, and he handed me an envelope with $100 and a plane ticket. He warned me not to run because he'd have to come looking for me. I assured him that I wasn't going anywhere, I was just glad to be out of jail. The airplane ticket was for Cleveland so that told me it was my friends who took care of me.

The trial started up and my buddies who were involved and I had a meeting about what to do. McGilvray hadn't been indicted yet, but they were going to indict him because he got away in one of the trucks with a friend of mine, Russell Kook. They wanted the plane crash.

Later on in life, he told me he was watching the plane burn as they were driving away and he was crying because he thought we were all dead. I don't blame him one bit for taking off because the wreckage of that plane, to anyone who was just pulling up to it, would look like there should be no survivors. I didn't expect them to stand around and wait for me. It was time to take off and take care of yourself. McGilvray and Russell got away to Madison, Wisconsin. And more power to them. Eventually, McGilvray was indicted, but then went on the run for 30 years. He's free now and I never ratted him out. I didn't snitch.

Should I have snitched? I can't really answer that because I don't think it would have done any good to anyone. I did what I did because I wanted to protect my friends. After all, I put the deal together. I'm not a snitch.

The trial went on and it became something of a circus. It cost both sides a lot of money. We ended up renting a house and living in Charleston to be nearer to everything going on. My lawyer, Richard Chosid, came from Detroit and lived with me, too. It became a full-time job. Richard had t-shirts made that said "survivor" with a map of Charleston, West Virginia on it. He also had little buttons made because one of the prosecutors, Wayne Rich, was complaining to the judge about what dangerous men we were. The buttons were mocking Wayne Rich about that and they said "It's only marijuana, Wayne."

Everybody laughed because it was, in fact, only marijuana. You would've thought that we were killers by the way he was talking about us. Judge Knapp was totally on the side of the prosecution at the time. This judge had us come back into his quarters at times, you know, to try to make deals. That's not supposed to happen during a trial. Good old boy stuff.

The trial continued on and on. We ran out of money, so we had to move out of the house we were renting. We ended up renting a space just outside of town in Kanawha State Forest and we lived in tents. My lawyer, Richard, sprung for a motorhome. That's where we lived. We got dressed at the forest and took showers at the outdoor showers. There was an article in one of the Charleston newspapers about our whole living situation. We made the best of our situation, too. We barbecued, smoked pot, drank, went to court every morning, went out for cocktails after court in local places in downtown Charleston. We became friends with a lot of the locals because we were living there. Nobody hated us. I mean, we were just a bunch of pot smugglers, none of us were really dangerous.

As it turned out, one of the investigators for Kagen, Harry Lee Shelor, Jr., was a bad guy.

During the trial, we eventually had to leave the state forest. So I went to Kentucky — it's the only place I could go — with Steve Riddle and his old lady, Pat Diehl. I was basically out of money and I needed a way to earn. We thought about more smuggles, but eventually settled on doing our own grow operation.

I got a phony ID — my alias was Thomas Cart, and we started looking for land. Ed Kagen had a piece of property in Kentucky that he had just sold and it had a little valley in it. It was prime real estate for growing marijuana. Somehow he got the guy who just bought it to sell it back to him. Kagen handled the paperwork for us, and I bought it back under my alias. I just signed some papers and we did a cash deal. All of a sudden we had 160 acres in the middle of Kentucky, outside of Brownsville in Edmonson County. My friend, Marshall Mechanik, who was also one of the defendants in my trial, was already familiar with growing marijuana. He showed me how to sex the plants so I could propagate efficiently.

We ended up with a really nice patch.

I didn't live on the property, though. I lived in a little town called Austin. I started up a dog kennel called Good Nature Kennels for something to keep me busy. I was jogging over by Big Bear State Park. I got to be pretty cool with all the local people and my neighbors, Mamie and Travis Watson.

Now, these people were back hill people, believe me. I mean, they had just gotten rid of their outhouse maybe a couple years before. They had been using an outhouse and pumping their own water.

I rented this little tiny house up on the hill, and I had to go past their house to get to it. My driveway was about a mile and a half long, and I had a little cottage with a barn. That's where I set up the dog kennels. I probably had 19 rottweilers and some bouviers. I had a lot of dogs. That was my cover and Steve and Pat went to the farm in an adjoining county about 40 minutes away. That's the farm where we were growing, and I would go back and forth to that and sex the plants. That was my job. Pat and Steve lived at the front of the property in a trailer. We got a few cattle to make it look like a legit farm.

We gave Harry Shelor, Kagen's investigator, the task to sit out in the field and make sure nobody discovered it, and if they did to let us know. Well, I guess Harry had a lot of hang-ups because he was wearing camouflage clothes and I thought he was a little goofy. He liked to play with guns and stuff— I hate guns, by the way. Back there on the property, I figured he was harmless, right? I told him if anyone came on the property, just get the fuck out and call to let us know. I told Harry, "No violence Harry!"

We agreed that he would run and we'd pick him up wherever he was, and then we'd just abandon the operation because I bought it on a bullshit name. We were paying Harry $50,000 because we ended up having 1,300 huge marijuana plants. I mean, the size of Christmas trees! At $1,000 a pound and close to a thousand pounds and we were sitting on a pretty profit. We were all going to live happily ever after. But you know what they say…the best laid plans of mice and men…

I was volunteering for all of the farmers in the area near Austin. I donated my time because I was growing pot and I told them I didn't need the money, but I'd be glad to help my neighbors because that's a big thing in Kentucky, helping your neighbors. Now, these people were wonderful people, too, by the way. God's people, for sure. I had a hen house and Mamie and Travis showed me how to kill my chickens. Mamie wore a floppy hat and, I mean, they were characters right out of a mountain picture. I enjoyed those people very much.

It's time for us to harvest and I asked a friend of mine named Donny "Skivvies" Bates and his girlfriend from Cleveland, Ohio to come to help. I had previously traded one of my rottweiler puppies to a girl from Lexington in exchange for two tickets to the Kentucky Derby. Her grandmother owned seats and I had always wanted to go.

I invited Skivvies to go with me and we had a great time. I had a couple grand with me in my boot and I wanted to bet on a horse named Woodchopper because I had spent the winter months chopping firewood to feed my wood burning stove up in that tiny cabin I lived in.

Now, this was in, I believe, 1981. I wanted to bet heavy on Woodchopper, but the odds were 30:1. Skivvies told me I'd had too many mint juleps to think Woodchopper would win.

Here we go again. I am drunk on my ass at the Kentucky Derby, snorting cocaine, partying away, full of shit again. Skivvies told me I was crazy to bet all of my money on that horse with those odds and he wouldn't let me do it.

I ended up betting half my money, but we're still screaming and yelling, having a damn good time.

I noticed this really beautiful girl sitting nearby with extremely long black hair. At that time, you know, I was hustling women. So I went over and talked to her, introduced myself, and she told me her name was Desiree. She gave me her phone number and I found out that she lived in Clearwater, outside of the Tampa area. I told her I'd get a hold of her sometime and maybe she could come and visit me in Kentucky. She told me that sounded nice and she loved the woods and all that. Of course I was playing it up that I had a dog kennel, trying to be an extra cool guy. I ended up winning, like, $9,000 but I had another $1,000 that I wanted to bet in my boot, and Donny Bates wouldn't let me. When the horses crossed the line, Woodchopper came in second and Skivvies about had a heart attack. Actually, so did I.

I said, "You motherfucker. I could have had that money on that horse." Thirty-to-one odds! Well, it might have been a long shot but I felt it in my gut. I wish I had paid attention to the feeling in my gut about Harry and his guns, to tell you the truth.

Steve and Harry developed some feud and I don't know what even started it. They fought all the time, arguing about the pot field, Steve complained that Harry's doing this or that wrong, Harry's complaining that Steve isn't feeding him well enough. At one point, Steve claimed Harry was looking at his woman who was sunbathing topless. I'm trying to control these little idiots, attempting to keep the peace. I'd say, "You know, guys, you don't have to be friends or anything. Once this is done, we can go separate ways, let's just finish the pot field, you know?" I kept tensions down for a while.

We're getting close to the harvest and I had previously gotten in touch with Desiree. I invited her down and told her I'd pick her up at the Tennessee border which wasn't far from the airport. You know, I enticed her with my dog kennel and she was a beautiful girl. Boy was she in for the time of her life, because this is a straight girl. I mean, you've got to understand that she's out of her element with us. We made the arrangements for me to pick her up.

Before I left, I told Harry that he could have a marijuana plant for himself to hang up and, you know, dry it out. He could go ahead and smoke some. It's only one plant and it was a tiny one. One plant out of 1,300 mature plants. To a rational person, that should be no big deal. I guess Steve wasn't rational because he had found him with that plant hung up and he went completely nuts on Harry.

I was like, "Woah, woah, woah, Steve, come on, man. It's just one marijuana plant, what are you talking about?" Steve and Harry are both throwing insults and slurs saying, "Motherfucker this", "motherfucker that". Harry's probably 20 yards away from Steve; I'm standing halfway between them trying to settle them down. I told Steve I'd pay him for the plant. I wanted him to forget it, get over it. Well, he's stubborn and wouldn't let it go. He kept pushing Harry and calling him a dumb motherfucker. Harry snapped. He whipped out his pistol and aimed it at Steve. Steve said, "What are you going to do, shoot me, Harry?

Harry said, "Yeah" and shot him.

The bullet hit him in the thigh but it went through one leg and into the next, just missing his nuts. My heart was going to jump right out of my chest. Skivvies' girlfriend, Karen, poor girl, was watching all of this go down. I mean, this was a surprise attack, believe me.

Steve kept yelling, "You motherfucker, you shot me." Harry was still pissed and he charged Steve with the pistol directly pointed at him, and he got right up on him and he said, "Now I'm going to kill you."

I was trying to keep pace with Harry and I pushed his arm up in the air when he leveled it at Steve. I said, "Harry, what in the fuck are you doing? Don't do this Harry." He was pale white and shaking, he had his fatigues on and his military boots. I mean, it was a sight to see now that I look back at it, and he's trembling and Steve's still cursing him out, and I'm telling Steve to shut up because Harry was going to shoot him, maybe even kill him! He already had shot him once, what's a second time to Harry? Steve's pretty stupid, to be honest with you. Here we got a million dollars worth of marijuana — a misdemeanor in Kentucky — and now we got a gun battle to deal with, okay? I'm totally disappointed in these yo-yo's and I was a yo-yo for hanging around with these yo-yo's, let's get that straight.

I succeeded in talking Harry out of shooting Steve again. That was one step in the right direction here. There's a creek that ran along the property from the front to the back where we grew the marijuana.

As we're walking along the creek, I said, "Steve, we got to get you to a hospital" and then I told Harry to walk next to me. Poor little Karen was with us, too. Damn, she just came down to help harvest some marijuana and now she witnessed a gun shooting. We're getting down to the creek and Steve started up with Harry again, "I'm going to get you for this, you motherfucker."

I said, "Steve, shut up, you're not going to get anyone." Harry's walking behind me and he's ready to shoot him again. I stopped Harry again, and said, "No more shooting. We got to harvest this pot. This is going to be hard enough to get away with as it is, because now there's going to be a gunshot wound reported because Steve has to go to the hospital."

Anytime somebody shows up at a hospital with a gunshot wound, the cops are contacted. I don't care if it's an accidental shooting and you shot yourself. The cops have to come, okay? Anyway, we made it to the trailer where Pat was and Steve told her what happened. Now she starts in on Harry. "Motherfucker Harry!" Steve and Pat are hillbillies, okay?

Harry still wanted to shoot Steve at this point, but we got Steve out of there. I told Pat to go to the hospital and tell them that she and Steve were both walking in the woods at my dog kennel, and Steve felt a sting and you heard a gunshot. I told her not to say anything about the marijuana property.

We agreed that she would drive back to my dog kennel, because those cops weren't going to buy this story. But, honestly, it didn't matter if they didn't buy it. They had to be able to prove it. As long as they didn't come near the marijuana field, it's okay. I emphasized that fact that, under no circumstances should she come back to that property.

Well, guess what? Pat decided she was going to pop back just for a minute to give the dogs water. Well, two detectives, Daryl Phelps and another cop who was with him, were investigating the shooting and they followed her after she left the hospital. They got out of their car and started nosing around, okay? So they're tromping through the woods and, well, I'm pretty sure you can guess what they discovered.

They followed the creek and came up on the marijuana field. They saw the tent that Harry had been living in, all that marijuana growing, plus you could smell that shit, okay? These were mature plants. These were going to be harvested any day.

They approached the tent and called out for whoever was in the tent to come out. Harry had a rifle, you know—he had his guns back there. Harry just lost it, I guess, and opened fire on them. There was a gun battle and Detective Daryl Phelps tried to take cover behind a tree. Harry shot him before escaping.

Supposedly, Harry set the tent on fire but not everything burned because they found one of my Good Nature Dog kennel cards. Daryl Phelps was airlifted out, but he later died of his wounds. I'm very sorry about that and I didn't have anything to do with it. I don't really know how to even tell anybody, his children or anything that I'm just so terribly sorry for what happened that day. I know there is nothing I can say to ease their pain, but I continue to pray for Detective Phelps and his family to this day.

This is what happens when you're fooling around in criminal games and there's guns around, that's all I can say. You know there are prices to pay for being a dumb ass and this was somebody's life. I'm haunted by what happened every single day of my life, even after all these years.

This all went down while I was getting Karen out of there, and then I had to pick up Desiree from Tennessee, right? I had no idea Harry had gone nuts and committed murder. So Desiree and I are back at my little place watching television, the news, in fact.

Guess what comes on the news? My marijuana farm and information that a state patrol officer was shot and killed. I had never told this girl anything about the marijuana field. She was just there because she was into the rugged lifestyle. I switched the TV off and tried to make myself appear calm and normal. Inside, though, I'm flipping out because I had learned that somebody got killed and I knew Harry did it. That's a very sick feeling to have in your heart at the time. I put on the charade and we go to bed. The house is real quiet and the dogs are put away. I got Charlie and Wendy in the house with me and something must've woken me because it was late. I don't know what time it was in the middle of the night, but I looked out my window.

My driveway was, I told you, a mile and a quarter long. After you got just past Mamie and Travis' house, you were at the very start of my entrance. It was an open dirt road. Well, here come more lights than I ever saw in my entire life. Not just a few, I'm saying the entire cavalry was coming.

They thought they were coming to the killer's house, because he had left my business card there and escaped. I got this poor girl in bed with me and she knows nothing about anything. Her world is about to be thrown upside down. She didn't know I was a marijuana grower or even that I was out on bond from the plane crash in Charleston. She knew nothing about my criminal activity.

She was about to find out, I can tell you that.

I know what all these lights coming down the driveway are all about. I saw the news clip, I knew who was coming. As they approached, I woke her up and said, "Now just lay here. I'm going to have to go outside, don't get scared, don't come running out. This is going to be a bad scene."

She sat up and didn't know what was happening or how to act because this girl was a straight girl. She didn't even smoke pot. She had no idea who she was laying in bed with.

I'll tell you who she was in bed with: Mr. Dumb Ass, that's who.

They pulled up in front and they've got the front of my cottage surrounded, like, in a horseshoe. Spotlights are all over my house and my dogs start going completely bananas. They were guard dogs and they were mean looking things. I threw on a pair of jeans before I walked out the front door. No shirt, no shoes. All I could see were lights and weapons pointed right at me.

"Down, down, you motherfucker, down!" and I was still walking with my hands over. They yelled, "Get the dogs or we'll shoot" — the dogs had come out behind me — "Get the dogs, we'll shoot the dogs." I'll admit that these cops showed some pretty great restraint, they're professional guys, I'll say that. I mean, they could have just opened up on those dogs, or me because I didn't have my hands totally over my head yet. It was a touchy situation. They're looking for a cop killer for God's sake. This isn't a fucking playground here. This is some real shit that took place. You also got to remember that the guy that got dusted in that marijuana field, he was also their friend.

This was August 7, 1981 and I'll never forget it. I was totally ashamed, scared, hurt. I mean, I was feeling so many emotions going through me at that time I can't even explain what it was like. I knew somebody had lost their life and I already felt guilty about what happened. I felt somewhat responsible for my bad judgment with Harry. They let me walk my dogs to the kennel. You better believe they walked with me, dozens of guns trained on me the whole time. This was a combined effort with, like, 30 to 40 state troopers, city police, and county sheriffs. I later found out that they had sent in snipers prior to driving up my road, and they set up in the trees too. These guys were not there to fuck around. They were there to kill somebody—me, actually, because their initial reaction was that I killed Detective Phelps.

They asked if anybody else was in the house. I said there was a girl in there and they told me to get her out. With my hands folded behind my back and down on my knees, I called for Desiree to come outside. I assured her that the cops would not harm her.

Poor Desiree is as white as snow, scared to death. She came out and they put handcuffs on her and took her into custody. I told them no one else was in the house. No dogs, no nothing. They went inside and swept the whole house. This is as serious as anything you could ever see, believe me, and these guys handled themselves well. I didn't blame them at all. All I could think was, *Fucking Harry.*

I mean, I was pissed.

They put me in the back of a squad car and started interrogating me, and I told them "I don't know anything about a marijuana field." I was doing my thing, you know, "I don't know what you're talking about," playing the criminal, claiming I really wasn't a criminal, but we all know I was. I'm not going to tell them anything, but I do tell them the girl had nothing to do with anything, you know, she's completely innocent, man. She came here to visit me from Florida. She actually didn't know a damn thing. They said, "Well, you're in a lot of trouble now and we have a dead state trooper. We found your business card there and you've got some talking to do right now or you're going to have more serious problems than you ever imagined, Mr. Lill."

I said, "Well, I can't really say anything. I need to talk to an attorney."

They said, "You won't be talking to an attorney" then they got out of the car; there were three of them. Two in the front seat and one in the back with me. They got out of the car and had a huddle. I'm sitting in the back, handcuffed. A decision of some kind was made because all of the cars and the ambulances turned off the flashing lights, and drove out of the driveway quietly. They just drove out, down the one road, real quiet, and then I was there with three guys. They took the girl away too. And the one guy was missing a finger. He was in the back seat, and he looked at me, and he said, "Mr. Lill, you're going to escape right now." He reached over, opened my door, and he kicked me into the dirt. "You're escaping now," and he had his cocked pistol aimed at me.

"Wait a minute, wait a minute, wait a minute," I said, immediately realizing what was happening. "I am no cop killer, and I know who did it and I can help you get him, but I'm not a killer. I didn't do it."

I also told them I was out on bond for the Charleston deal. I told them that if the Feds got notice of this, my ass was grass. I needed them to want to make some kind of deal with me. I actually wanted to help them catch Harry. All I did was grow marijuana, I explained, and I never expected anything like this. They listened to me and they said, "So, how do you think you're going to get him?"

I said, "I know he's going to call me. He'll call me because he doesn't have anybody else to call. But I have to have some kind of assurance that I get to walk. I can't be charged with anything."

They agreed, "Okay, we're going to see what we can do" and they let me back in the car. We drove to the state trooper post, and then I told them on the way there that Harry was going to call me soon, so we needed to get this done quickly, whatever it was that we were going to do.

I insisted on documentation as an assurance that they weren't going to tell the DEA or the Federal government about me growing this pot because, if they did, I might as well just be shot because I'll do 20 more years. I actually said that to those cops because my life was on the line, thanks to Harry.

We arrived at the state police station and a helicopter came, and it's the governor's aide, and they give me immunity. We got right to work because I told them there's no time to cock around. I knew he's going to be looking for me first because he wouldn't think that the cops were onto me. He's so stupid he probably didn't even know he left my business card there for anyone to find.

I got my documentation that I wouldn't be connected in any way to this fiasco. We took off and went back to my little cottage up on the hill where snipers were waiting in the trees again because he might be coming there. I really thought he'd call before he showed up.

We're sitting there, and I had Jack Daniels, naturally, because I'm an alcoholic. Not to mention, I was pretty hyped up. So I asked them if I could have a drink, and they said, "Yeah, you can have a drink, but don't get drunk." So I poured a Jack Daniel's and we're just sitting there waiting for hours. We just talked and basically the conversation kept turning back to what a dangerous motherfucker Harry was.

I told them that I didn't know he was that dangerous, but he obviously was because he shot Steve and the cop on the same day. These guys were cool guys. I'm going to say that, and I'll never forget them.

I will say that they wanted him, and believe me, they wanted his ass bad. I had a '50s pickup truck, a green one, and that's what I used for my kennel. We started making all these plans on how, if he calls me, we're going to catch him. I said, "Harry is obviously going to have a shoot out with you, because he's probably got that same pistol he carried that he shot Steve with." It was a nine millimeter semi-auto, I believe.

We came up with this plan: They wanted to lay two guys down in the bed of my truck and meet him somewhere. I said, "I don't think so — you're going to have a shootout and somebody could get hurt." Here I am trying to think like a cop, believe or not. I'm using whatever criminal expertise I have to figure out this movie script we got going. Anyway, ding-a-ling-a-ling, phone rings.

Guess who? Harry.

I said, "Harry, what the fuck? Do you know you killed a cop?"

He laughed — *the fucker actually laughed* — and he said, "Yeah, I know." I mean, he thought it was fucking funny and he was proud of it. I could hear it over the phone. That was the last thing I expected.

I said, "I got to get the fuck out of here because they're going to be onto me. I've got to get out of here now. So what do I do? Do you want me to meet you, pick you up? What do you want me to do?" I was acting like I was nervous, panicked, unsure of what was going to happen next. Well, I guess that was all pretty true, but he believed that I was being genuine.

He said, "Yeah, I'll call you back again in a little while, and I'll tell you where I am and we can meet."

I said, "Okay, call me back because I got to get the fuck out of here. The cops are going to come here, Harry and you're going to have my ass in grass. Hurry up."

We all sat back down. Now everybody is biting at the bit because he made the contact, you see. We're talking about how to do it, and I said, "Do you guys know anywhere off the 65" — I think that was the highway — "that we could meet where you have connections and where there's a small gas station?" I came up with this idea! I guess I would make a pretty good detective, right?

"I'll drain gas out of my truck, and we'll get it close to empty, but we'll leave enough in it so I can get to where we're going. And when I get Harry in the truck, I'll tell him I'm going to run out of gas, so we have to get gas. Harry will look at the fuel, okay? I know he will, so we have to drain the gas out."

They all thought that was a decent plan and we drained the gas out of my truck. Harry called back, told me about this hotel, I think it was a Quality Inn or something on the highway. He said, "I'll find you. You park and I'll find you."

I said, "Okay, Harry. Get in the truck when I get there because we got to get going. Don't be dicking around. Don't make me ride around, because I can't get arrested for this." I sounded pretty real to be honest with you. But we're talking about catching a killer, so this is no fucking game, okay? I mean real bullets, not play. Fucking scary shit, and I'm surprised I didn't have a heart attack while this was going on.

We all loaded up, ready to roll. Now these guys all made arrangements ahead of time. They got maps out while this is all getting ready to go. They had a connection who had a little Phillips 66 station, some kind of little bum-fuck gas station in the middle of nowhere. They were going to set themselves up there, and I was going to take a specific road because it was really close to this hotel. I repeated the plan to the cops so we all were sure everything would go smoothly. I reminded them that Harry was a private investigator and he would be looking for cops, so they had to set up out of sight. I was determined to get him in my possession, and take him to those cops on a silver fucking platter, believe me. I wanted them to have him. I didn't like Harry and I was very sorry at the loss of life. They were cool, they trusted me.

I pulled up to the Quality Inn, and I'm sitting in the parking lot just waiting, constantly looking at my watch. All of a sudden Harry's face appears at my driver's side window. He scared the piss out of me. He's wearing overalls and a baseball cap. Harry used to have a beard but he was completely clean shaven now. He went around to the passenger side and got in the car, and I said, "I hope to God you don't got no fucking gun or anything on you, Harry."

He said, "No, I don't have a gun," but I didn't believe him.

I said, "You don't got a gun?" I was questioning him about that, and he said he didn't but I'll never know for sure now.

You got to understand, I'm hanging around with a fucking killer and he could kill me. After I look at everything now, he could have easily killed me when I stopped him from shooting Steve. This guy was already bonkers. He shot Steve and now he's killed a cop, so he's not above killing me, that's for sure.

The gas station was maybe a mile or so away, and it seemed like it took a year to get there. As we drove, he told me that he had stolen a vehicle, broke into a house, grabbed some clothes, and shaved his face. He was trying to stay out of sight and under the radar. I glance at my fuel indicator — for show, you know — and I say, "Harry, I got to get some gas, and there's a sign over there." I see this big sign like an old fashioned Phillips 66. "I'll go over there."

I know these cops are set up there and they're posing as gas station attendants. They've cleared the area, and I know this shit is going to go down now. I'm also contemplating maybe bang, bang, bang, okay? I opened my door, and got out to pay for the gas. I'm nervous that my back is to Harry because I know he's out of his mind right now, but I play it cool. I got about three feet from that truck, and those fucking cops came from everywhere under the sun with their guns out, and they were on him like flies on shit. They had their guns poked in his ears, his nose, everywhere on his body. These guys practiced the most restraint I could imagine, because he just killed their friend.

Now, dig this, man. I wouldn't have blamed them for gunning him down and accidentally shooting me, because I was that mad at myself, if you could understand that. This whole thing was just nasty.

They got his ass, and they weren't that nice to him when they drug him out of the car, needless to say. I wouldn't expect them to be either. I mean, how the fuck else should they have acted? One of the cops who was there, it was his best friend who was killed — his partner was gone. He walked me around the side of the gas station and he put his arm around me, and he said, "We both lost some stuff today."

Now this is one helluva good cop, because the thing had upset me. I had tears in my eyes over this. I still get them, to be honest with you, because a nice family man lost his life over a fucking pot field. See, nobody should lose their life over marijuana or go to jail for it either.

We had to go back to the state police post to complete some paperwork. Harry is now in custody and a lot of people are relieved about that. I was at the post for quite a while and Daryl Phelps' wife, who was there because she had been told that he had been captured, hugged me and squeezed me really tight. I mean, she made me cry. She wasn't mad at me, I could tell. She actually thanked me because she knew I helped catch the sucker.

Did I do the wrong thing? You tell me. I don't know, I mean I had to do something because this guy was off balance. He wouldn't stop killing. He was just a bad guy. I thought I was hanging with a private eye for a lawyer, and he ended up being a cop killer. Later, I come to find out, Harry had killed somebody else before—stabbed them. Knowing who he really was doesn't make things any easier, I'll tell you that much. I don't think I'll ever get over it.

Now it's time to let Jerry go, because that was the deal. Now in the house, they had found some guns, and confiscated them along with a white Oldsmobile that I used for cruising around taking pot back and forth across the country. They gave me the keys to the car, opened my trunk and threw the guns in there. They told me to get rid of those guns because I wasn't supposed to have them. Then they shook my hand and said, "Now, you're going to be available to us this week?"

I said, "Yes, sir."

The other cop patted me on the back and he said, "If you ever want a job, you've got one." I should've taken that job, looking back now. I made a helluva detective that night.

I'm confident I did the right thing by helping the cops get Harry. There are, without a doubt, certain criminals in this world who think he's a hero for shooting a cop, but he's not. He's a piece of shit.

I actually forgive Harry, too, because this is part of my own healing and recovery. Somehow the Devil got in that asshole somewhere in his life, and he went the wrong way. I don't really know what else to say about that because I can't hate him but I get angry about what he did.

It's hard to hate someone who you know was pulled the wrong way by the Devil, but I can hate his actions. Anger erupts in me when I think about what he did, but maybe he was dealt a bad hand in life and just fell off the path. I know he fell off the path because I believe we are all born good. We're born as loving, caring humans. Somewhere that can get buried by greed, loss, pain, and substance abuse only buries those qualities even deeper.

CHAPTER SIX

I Won't Back Down

I was released from Charleston on bond, but I was still under
investigation. Now it's time for me to reorganize, because I've
got to make money. I lost a lot of investment in the DC-6 crash so I
need to hit the ground running, and the only way I know how to
make money is doing what I do best.

You know what I'm talking about: moving marijuana.

Of course I still had a lot of connections so I headed towards
Cleveland, Ohio.

I knew a guy up there I had done business with before and my
lawyer, Richard Chosid, had introduced me to a fella in Florida
named John Cole. I also had met a guy, David Franklin, in
Kentucky, so I had access to marijuana all around the country. I just
had to figure out where I was going to sell it.

I got my dogs out of the kennel – Charlie and Wendy. I knew a
guy who used to work for a veterinarian in Parma, Ohio, and he

took care of my dogs when I needed him. I decided to leave Wendy with him, and I took Charlie with me. He travelled around with me, guarded my money, sat in the back seat with me when I brought pot back and forth between Michigan and Florida. They were well-trained and great watch dogs.

Charlie was at my house where I had run this DC-6 deal out of. I had put the telephone in his full official name — Charles Holenhaus.

Well, Charles Holenhaus, a.k.a. Charlie—my dog—was indicted. There was a federal indictment for him and they were actively looking for him with an arrest warrant!

They had gone to see my landlord in Siesta Key, Florida, on North Shell Road, Bobby Burns. Bobby became a good friend of mine more and more throughout the years, and they brought Bobby in to question him.

Well, Bobby told them that he had met a short guy named Charlie, kind of a stubby fellow; he thought he spoke German but he wasn't really sure if that was the guy. They showed him some pictures but good ol' Bobby couldn't identify him. They really wanted Charles Holenhaus because they assumed he was the lead in this job due to the telephone being in his name.

I'm still under investigation and so are a lot of people. I applied for certiorari — a writ seeking review of a lower court decision by a higher court — to the United States Supreme Court so, legally, I'm tied up but free on appeal bond. This is cool because it means I can activate across the country.

Permission to travel between Florida and Detroit was granted because my lawyer was in both Florida and Detroit. There are a lot of stops between Florida and southeastern Michigan, which means I had a lot of potential outlets for my old business venture.

I received immunity and a subpoena to testify in front of a federal grand jury, so I went to Charleston, West Virginia. I immediately got a hold of my lawyer, Richard Chosid—good lawyer, good guy. He protected me a lot.

In front of the federal grand jury, I was questioned about the elusive Charles Holenhaus. During this time period, I was traveling in a Ford F250 with a camper top on the bed. Charlie and Wendy were in the back with my camper top on when I went in for a hearing with the federal grand jury. My lawyer briefed me a little bit, as any good lawyer would, and he told me I had to answer the questions because they gave me immunity.

I tried to figure out how I'm going to answer these questions without ratting anybody out. They wanted to know about a guy named Craig Bruce McGilvray; they wanted to know a bunch of names, some of which I had never heard. They were really concentrating on Charles Holenhaus, though. I just lead them down the road and play the game. They asked me if I knew the whereabouts of Charles Holenhaus. I told them, "Yes, I do."

Tim DiPiero, the prosecutor, said, "You know where he is?"

I said, "Yes, I do."

"Can you tell us where?"

I said, "Well, he's here in Charleston, West Virginia, right now."

DiPiero was shocked, "Charles Holenhaus is here right now?

"Yes, he is, sir."

Of course they wanted to find him and they had more questions, so when they asked, my responses were along the lines of, "Not to my recollection," or "Not to the best of my knowledge." I wasn't giving them straight answers, just toying with the government. I wasn't lying to them either because I didn't want any perjury charges. I avoided everything and repeated the fact that I couldn't remember or asked them to repeat questions.

I did that for hours. When we did get back to Charles Holenhaus, they asked me to produce Charles Holenhaus, and I said, "Well, I really don't know if you want me to do that."

They said, "Why is that?"

I said, "Well, he's out in the parking lot, he's in my truck."

They said, "Charles Holenhaus is in your truck right now?"

I said, "Yeah, Charles Holenhaus is my dog."

The prosecutor threw his pencil up in the air and said, "Oh, God." The grand jury kind of snickered because they were looking for a dog and Charlie wasn't the guy they were going to get.

They were pretty humiliated about that and I soon went on my way, back out into the streets to do what I do: sell marijuana across the United States.

You know, even to this day, I believe marijuana can be a positive drug. Marijuana is legal in Michigan now and medical marijuana is legal across the country, which is about time. I used it for medication, to calm myself.

I mentioned previously that I was manic depressive, and marijuana helped me. The problem with me was that I mixed a lot of stuff with it. I just wanted to party, but now I know better.

Like I said, I had to regroup. I started running with a new gang out of Florida who I met through my lawyer, Richard. He had been buying shrimp boats and leasing them through my friend, Johnny Cole; his girlfriend, Mishelle; Dennis Hausdorf — a whole new group. They were hanging out in Sarasota and renting houses all over the place, too. Johnny was getting Jamaican weed and running around with little Mishelle — who ended up being my old lady down the road.

She was probably one of the nicest, most beautiful human beings that I had ever met in my life.

Mishelle-y — *Shelly Belly.* She had balls the size of a rhinoceros…metaphorically speaking. This girl was as brave as could be. She would do anything and was loyal as hell. Johnny was her old man at the time, but he had a mistress down in Ft. Lauderdale so she and I were hooking up.

On the business side of things, I moved pot all across the country from Johnny and his gang. I had a whole new group of smugglers and actually started making big money again. I had lawyer bills to pay, remember, because I'm going to the United States Supreme Court.

So now my lawyer, Richard Chosid—in the middle of all this—was busted by the Feds.

This is not good for me because I have money tied up in this guy for my own legal issue. He had leased the Johnny Cole group a shrimp boat to move marijuana — 30,000 pounds of marijuana. It got busted off the coast of Louisiana.

I get a phone call from Richard that he can't represent me any more because he'd just been arrested. I had previously given him a down payment to file my appeal. I said, "Well, what about my money?" He said, "I had to use that for my lawyer."

That was the end of Richard as my attorney.

Actually, Richard pleaded guilty to smuggling marijuana with this group. Before I even went to jail, my lawyer went to jail, which is kind of unusual. Since I still had not been granted my certiorari to the United States Supreme Court yet, I needed to gather more funds to pay for a new lawyer whom I hired in Wisconsin.

I bought a cottage with another friend of mine in Portage, Wisconsin, and we were going to use that as a stash house. Johnny's bringing me weed and things are going super, super good. They had some Jamaican pot left from this one deal that they couldn't get rid of. Some of it was in Dayton, Ohio with a buddy of mine named Big Don, who was also part of their group.

Some of the pot was stashed in Bradenton, Florida. They were going to sell it to me cheap, like, $150 a pound. I could get $250 a pound so I was thrilled with that deal. I was making a ton of money. I shipped some to Wisconsin and stashed it in the cottage we had on the lake up in Portage. Mishelle and I would go back and forth between Florida and Wisconsin, and I also had drivers taking it across the country.

One of my drivers, Bobby Zingg, became a very good friend of mine. I looked him up years later and found out he suffered from depression, alcoholism, and pain pills. Committed suicide—blew his brains out. There goes another one of my fallen angels.

When you live a lifestyle like this, you slowly kill yourself; you're slowly killing your family, your friends. You hurt a lot of people. You may not understand it in the moment, but you are to blame for all of the pain and suffering. You can't blame anybody else but yourself for the things that happen around you.

It took me a long time to realize that the first place to look for a scapegoat is in the fucking mirror. Only one person stares back at you, so take full responsibility for your actions, good or bad.

I had given a guy named Rick 700 pounds of Jamaican marijuana and had loaded it in this van that was small enough to drive into a storage unit that I rented at a place called You Store It.

This is another one of those times when I know God is truly looking out for us. Because I knew the Feds were watching me, I needed Rick to be my front man.

I was also trying to keep a lid on this guy, Greg McCafferty, because I had a feeling he was a loose cannon, and the cops were harassing him. We were afraid he was going to just break open and tell everything about another friend of mine.

So, in the interim of trying to make money and keep an eye out, and baby sit, I was doing these deals with all this extra Jamaican marijuana. I mean, I had to make a living, you know, no doubt about it. I told Rick to never go near this marijuana, just leave it in the van and I would come and take care of it. Just leave it alone.

I continued to do my business while I waited for the right time to pick up the load in the van. Rick contacted me — well, he pages me because there were no cell phones yet — and told me that he's been arrested for all that marijuana. I'm thinking, *Oh, shit, how did they find that pot?* Apparently, he wanted to get an ounce of marijuana for himself — I thought he was an idiot at the time — and they were watching him.

The cops told him that they didn't want him—they wanted me, Jerome Otto Lill—yours truly—and if he could set me up, they'd let him go. Little did they know he was already communicating with me. He was trying to help me not get caught because if I got cracked for this while I'm out on bond, well, that could end badly for me.

You've got to remember, I was out on bond for attempting to smuggle 26,000 pounds into the U.S. There was this DEA agent in Cleveland, Ohio, named McGooch who, along with his side-kick, Charlie Carter, wanted to catch Craig McGilvray so bad they could taste it. And they knew the way to get him would be to get me.

Those guys wanted me bad, let's put it that way, but he couldn't fucking have me, okay? I wasn't a bad guy. I wasn't a good guy, either, but this guy thought we were gangsters. We were just pot dealers, really.

At least, I was.

I sent Rick some money under the table and I paid for his lawyer to keep him on my side. The lawyer made a deal to set me up, and they were going to tap his phones, and he was going to lure me back to Cleveland.

Now this gets a little complicated because Rick hadn't made it clear to me what was going on, and they didn't know he had talked to me. This worked out really well because they made their signed deal with Rick's attorney, and then they tried to set me up. His phone was tapped when he called me to tell me to come to his place. He said, "You know, you've got to come and get the van."

I played dumb, "What van?"

He said, "You know, man, the van, with all the pot in it."

I said, "What do you mean, all the pot in it? I don't know anything about that. Rick, have you lost your mind?"

Rick was in on this with me. He was slick. He helped me out. And McGooch and them had to keep their deal with him and let him go. I just never went back to that kennel or anywhere near that place ever again. He lost me on that one.

McGooch messed with me at the airport one time, when I flew into Cleveland. I came off a flight at night and somehow they knew I was coming.

I came out of the Cleveland Hopkins Airport with an athletic bag slung over my shoulder and $10,000 in it. They dumped it all out right in front of the airport where you would pick up your baggage. Dumped it all over the ground, rousted me, just like in a movie. I wouldn't talk to him. He said, "What's all this money?"

I said, "That's my money to go pay my lawyer in Detroit, I'm just stopping here in Cleveland to say hi to a few people." I told him it was just "pocket change."

"That's kind of a lot of pocket change, isn't it, Jerome?"

I said, "Hey, man, my lawyer is expensive."

He didn't like me and I sure as hell didn't like him. I hate to spoil the story, but you know that sucker never got me.

I guess he was always just doing his job—he's got a role to play.

So after they let me go I ran through neighborhoods because I knew they were going to follow me. I cut through neighborhoods all over the Cleveland area on my way to the house from the airport. They couldn't follow me then. I also knew that, if I took a cab, they were sure to follow.

Yet again, I evaded their tactics.

CHAPTER SEVEN

Pirate Lives at 40

Now, moving money around back in those days was a lot easier when it was within the United States. I could fly into Sarasota, Florida for instance, from Cleveland, Ohio with a briefcase full of money. I flew in and out on Eastern Airlines a lot since they were the only ones that flew into Sarasota.

Sarasota was a very small airport, which made it convenient for a quick pop in on the red eye flight out of Cleveland. Sometimes I was the only one on the airplane. The stewardesses – flight attendants, to be more inclusive of men and women these days – would take me and set me up in first class for the whole trip. I sat there and drank wine and ate steaks, and they just kept bringing me stuff. They had no one else to serve.

In those days things were different. Metal detectors weren't being used, security checkpoints weren't in the way. I got off the airplane in Sarasota, and walked right into a little makeshift building with a conveyor belt for baggage. I'd grab my suitcase and jump right out into the parking lot. There was nobody around, period. So you could run around with money, drugs— it was loose as could be. Nothing like today, believe me. It was all pretty cool.

I bought a 1948 Galaxy — a 28 foot boat, which I kept down at the Casey Key Marina. She was named "China" and became my next vessel for smuggles. I pretended I was a pirate for a while — parrot and all.

Savage was my double yellow headed amazon parrot and he was always with me on China while I drank rum, waiting for a deal to come through. Well, one trip with China didn't turn out so well.

I knew this Australian sailor named Grubb. Grubb was going to travel out to Jamaica to load 1,200 pounds of marijuana, then head back. He took another sailor he knew on the trip with him, and Mishelle and I — she was my old lady by this point — waved goodbye to the boat from the inter-coastal bridge in Venice as it sailed off for Jamaica.

Remember that Mishelle used to be with Johnny Cole; it's not that we passed women around, it's just that we were a very tight-knit group of people—we had to be. We really couldn't trust other people, so if you broke up with your girlfriend, someone else would likely strike up a relationship. When you're living outside the law, you can't go outside your group. Mishelle and I just worked out, and there was no tension with the situation between Johnny and I.

While we were driving to the house after seeing off the China, we passed a goat farm. I pretty much bought Mishelle anything she wanted. She decided she wanted a goat so I stopped on the way to this new house we had rented and I bought her a pygmy goat. We named him Frisbee. Now, I've got Rottweilers in the backseat, a Chow named China (yes, the same name as the boat), and a goat named Frisbee, all in the backseat of my car. A clown car of pets and a funny sight to see looking in the rearview mirror.

We pulled up at our rental and decided this is where we're going to hang while we wait for the boat to come back, because those guys took their time. This house was in the Venice area, and we pulled up to see Jane, Grubb's old lady, waiting for us.

We waited and waited to hear word about how things were panning out. With no cell phones, everything was done by pay phone. We would get a message on a pager, go call back on a pay phone, and talk biz. You know the deal.

So, Grubb took China around the coast of Cuba when they were going through the Yucatan. Something must've been suspicious because they were followed by the Cuban Coast Guard and they opened fire on Grubb. He got hit in the leg and whoever his mate was — it was a big, fat guy out of Ft. Lauderdale — he got winged.

When they made it to Jamaica, the Jamaican women put mud on their wounds and patched him up. They stayed for about four or five days and the boat was loaded to head home. When they took off out of Jamaica, the Jamaican Coast Guard identified them as possible gun runners, so they popped them. It was just marijuana but they thought it was a gun running boat. Grubb and this guy got popped for that, and we got a phone call that the marijuana was confiscated.

So was the boat.

The Minister of Defense in Jamaica allowed us to buy it all back, minus the marijuana. He wanted to sell us the boat back for $25,000! Ernest, another boat captain, went down there. They had taken the radio navigation equipment and everything else that could be removed off the boat, but *they still wanted twenty-five grand?*

I said forget it.

They also wanted $50,000 to get Grubb and the other guy out of jail on a *ganja* fine. We ended up agreeing to that because I had to get Grubb home.

Now we're on the go. Mishelle and I had to move out of the house fast because, somehow, this could lead straight back to me. I had to be extra careful now because, remember, I'm out on bond for this DC-6 still. This whole time I've been waiting to go to the United States Supreme Court, running back and forth, trying to do appeals, trying to make money. And now I just lost my boat, a big down payment on this deal, my shipment of marijuana, and a $50,000 ganja fine to get my buddy out of a Jamaican jail.

It was not my finest day.

We did get them back home safe, however, and I went and got drunk again. In fact, I went on quite a long binge and got pretty sick when I withdrew from that phase — the DTs. You get *delirium tremens,* which is the official term for symptoms, and that can be pretty dangerous when you quit drinking too quickly, or go cold turkey. It can kill you. That alone should make a reasonable person know not to go on a binge and then quit like that, but I did it anyway. I dealt with loss — loss of money, loss of property, loss of friends — with more alcohol, I dug myself in deeper with all the abuse. It felt like loss after loss, and I dealt with it in very unhealthy ways.

The alcoholism for me kept getting progressively worse. Every year I was actually a bigger alcoholic than the last, to be perfectly honest. Eventually, I found that spirituality was what I needed to pull me out of the hole I was in. I prayed a lot; cleansed my soul before I could cleanse my physical body.

A lot happened before I could get to that point, however. One experience I had with Mishelle was a very dark place for me, and I am proud to say I pulled myself out of that despair. It's heavy— alcoholism— and even heavier when you pair it with grief. Mishelle and I were two peas in a pod when it came to alcoholism. Not a good pair in that regard.

You know things are bad when you keep drinking even though you get sick. Years back, I contracted swine flu and, let me tell you, I was sick as a dog; vomiting, diarrhea, the works. I ended up getting the DTs again, so the only logical solution for an alcoholic is to start drinking again. *How fucked up is that?* Any alcoholic will tell you that they'll take a drink of alcohol even if they know it's coming right back up. How disgusting is that? Go take a look in the mirror after that sometime. Just take a good long look in the mirror and you'll see what alcoholism looks like.

I'm sure you think I'm barking up the wrong tree, but if you really examine the situation, things can get gruesome when you fall into an alcoholism spiral. There is nothing glamorous about it. There will be a point in your life that you will have shit running down your leg or vomit on your shirt. This is the truth and, if you choose to drink, this is what you have to look forward to.

You may have started out as a good person, but it's the alcohol that changes you. It changes you into an asshole. Very simple. You know, it's the same thing with pills— Vicodin, heroin, all of it. Barbiturates— all that shit. You think you're finding a solution for all of your problems, but you're really just creating bigger problems. When you come out of it, you've destroyed more of yourself and hurt more people.

Hurt yourself!

Mental health plays a role, too, because sometimes people turn to alcohol to "check out" when they have mental health issues. That still doesn't solve the problem. Sure, it may be a temporary fix, but it's only causing long-term pain and grief. I was diagnosed as manic-depressive and was prescribed pills. That shit didn't work. So I decided to "drink" my pills. I thought I could drink my depression away. That shit didn't work either. Even if you think you have everything under control, sit back and think whether or not you're drunk right now. When was your last drink? It may be time to take a look in the mirror. Take responsibility for your actions.

As time went on, we got our money back together after we lost our boat, China. We decided we would buy another boat, a fishing boat. It was a nice boat with a tuna tower on it. Grubb and Ernest were back with us and we had new plans to smuggle marijuana out of Jamaica. Mishelle and I had another house, and an apartment complex called The Gulf and Pines over in Sarasota. Things were going pretty well for us.

Then, Mishelle gets pregnant. I find out I'm going to be a daddy while I'm still smuggling marijuana. Obviously it wasn't in the plans, but I have to figure out how I'm going to handle everything now. I mean, I had a lot going on. I've got a Egg Harbor Sport Fisherman down at a house in the Keys and a cabin up in Portage, Wisconsin; pot stashed that I need to get rid of; and now a kid on the way. Well, to add to it, Mishelle was put on bed rest because she had a high-risk pregnancy. So I got her a hospital bed and had it put in the apartment. She promised me she wouldn't drink or take drugs because she wanted this baby. I told her that I supported her and I would keep making money to support her and the baby. I told her to lay there and take care of herself and the baby.

I went to Madison, Wisconsin, and everybody was already starting to call me daddy; all my buddies that I was working with. "Jerry is going to be a father," they'd tease, and I was kind of getting into that, actually. The idea was growing on me. So I had to pick up, like, 150Gs in Madison.

I had an Igloo cooler that I stashed all the money in because it had a lid that would seal down nice and tight. Ernest and I are driving through Chicago in rush hour — the rush hour beltline, I think they called it — and I had the money and my dogs. I was a happy guy. I had a beautiful blue Chevy El Camino with a camper top over the back end. It was a great car, and perfect for driving with my dogs because they loved it in the back.

As we're moving through the Midwest, we hit a pretty bad snowstorm. The snow was coming down heavy and the wind was blowing hard. *Thud!* I looked in my rearview mirror and I watched my camper top flying down the median, and my Igloo cooler bouncing down the expressway.

Shit. I slammed on the fuckin' brakes and swung over into the median of the road because I was already driving in the left lane. Cars are swerving out of the way, you know, because I basically just came to an abrupt stop right in front of them. I have $150,000 bouncing down the interstate in a cooler. By this time I'm out of my car, my eyes are trained on the cooler because I don't want to lose sight of it in this snow. It finally finds a place to rest in the median. I ran down the median to get my cooler and it felt so good to pick that baby up and it was still sealed shut. That was a breath of relief, believe me.

The dogs are just standing in the back of my car, watching me. People driving by are looking at me like, What in the hell is he doing? With the cooler back in my possession, I ran back to the El Camino and I backed it all the way up to where my camper top landed. This is at rush hour in Chicago and I backed my car up against traffic.

That seems dangerous to me now, but I didn't care at the time. We popped the camper top back on, and I told Ernest to drive so I could hold the top on the car. Ernest pulled off at the next exit and we found a Shell station. I hired the guys there to put the top back on so it wouldn't come off.

See, I had it fixed with C-clamps, but one big gust of wind proved that method to be ineffective.

By the grace of God, again, I witnessed a miracle. To have a camper top fly off at oncoming traffic, an igloo cooler tumbles down the highway with cash and the lid stayed on, and no one was hurt. That's a miracle. That is God. And I'm going to insist upon that. That was a lot of excitement for my heart so Ernest and I stop and get a bottle of rum and a hotel for the night.

The next day, we decided to head back to Sarasota early. I wanted to surprise Mishelle and show her that I got the money to help pay for the doctors. The medical expenses were growing and we didn't have insurance so I had to pay for everything with cash. And the sky was the limit now, because I had my bread. Everything was cool. We still have a scam down in the Keys with Jamaica, but it was on hold because there were a lot of problems with it. I did, however, feel safer again, because I had $150,000 back in cash, plus I had some other money stashed. Rocking and rolling again, feeling good.

As I walked up the stairs, I heard giggling from inside our apartment. When I entered our place, I saw Mishelle sitting there with a girlfriend of hers, Gail. Gail drove for us at different times so she knew about what we did. On the table between them was a bottle of wine, and donuts were on Mishelle's nose.

"Donuts" happen when you snort cocaine; it creates a ring around the edge of your nostril, and it looks like a powdered donut ring. If you've been a coke tooter, you know about donuts. Well, the last thing I expected to see was a pregnant woman with a bottle of wine and donuts around her nose.

Needless to say, I was angry, extremely angry. I didn't really know what to say, and I got kind of vicious. "Mishelle, what are you doing?" I yelled.

She said, "Nothing. Gail and I are just talking, you know."

I said, "No, you're not just talking. Have you looked in the mirror lately?" She didn't know what I was talking about, so I grabbed her by the arm and I pulled her into the bathroom, and pointed at her nose in the mirror. "Two little white circles around them, that's dust. I ain't no fuckin' idiot, I know what the fuck you're doing." I just lost my temper.

The only thing I could do was dump out the wine and throw out the cocaine. That didn't really help my anger, and I kept telling myself to stay cool, be calm. She's four and a half months along by this time and I know drugs are not at all good for pregnant women. My worst nightmares came true because the next morning, Mishelle got up and said there was some blood on the bed. And I thought, *Oh, fuck.*

I took her to Sarasota Memorial Hospital and the doctors informed us that she had a miscarriage. The doctors suggested that it would be emotionally healing if we saw the baby, the fetus. I don't think it was emotionally healing, it wasn't good for me. That was a turning point for Mishelle and I. I mean, we still hung out together and we did business, but I lost something there. I was a very cold man after that.

In true Jerry fashion, bring on more drugs and alcohol to fix the pain. It's ironic, isn't it? I turned to the things that caused this miscarriage to happen. That's how sick in the head I was. It still didn't register with me that alcohol and drugs caused pain, suffering, and broke people apart.

The urge to do these things just continuously got in the way of our business, money, friendships, family, everything. Innocent babies die because people just can't stop the drugs and alcohol. I wish I was able to forgive Mishelle earlier because I regret the way things were left.

You know, part of the moral of this story is about forgiveness. Mishelle continued to be an alcoholic after losing the baby, and we had never really been together tight again. I never gave any affection or attention to her about what happened. I was being a real selfish piece of shit, it was me, me, me. Honestly, most of my life was always me, me, me, and I would drink and feel sorry for myself because of me, me, me.

That's part of the problem with substance abuse – alcoholism – it's selfish at its core. It always became about the way it made me feel, nothing to do with others. Alcoholics are very selfish people and, until we can forgive, others aren't going to forgive. Forgiveness is a major key to getting better, getting sober. You've got to learn to forgive people and not hold grudges against them, because a lot of what happens is the alcoholic's fault. I enabled all the drug abuse and alcoholism because I was a drug-smuggling piece of shit, and it's as simple as that.

I do blame myself, but not in a sorrowful way. Tragedies happen, and forgiveness is a major thing in the battle over hurting and killing yourself along with other people. You may not realize it, but you take a lot of people down while you're doing this to yourself.

Anyway, life continued on. Mishelle and I were never as close, but the smuggling, and trafficking, and moving pot around, that continued and the money still continued for quite awhile. We were beginning to phase out because the job we had planned with a man in Jamaica named Mr. Chin was stalled. Mr. Chin kept saying he needed more money, more money, and nothing happened after he got more money. We never did get that money back, none of it.

Time went on, Shelly moved off, and John Cole and I were doing our little things, trying to get more smuggles together and being a little successful with some, but not as much. Then Johnny and I moved down to Sanibel Island, and we were hanging there for quite awhile. Johnny would move off here and move off there. The business started to fade — we just weren't doing well as far as making money.

I had met up with one of his other partners named Dennis Hausdorf. Dennis and I hit it off. He owned a liquor store in St. Petersburg, Florida, called Parkin Starkey Liquors, and Dennis and I became immediate friends. I had basically decided that I wasn't going to do any business any more. I had gotten kind of numb to the whole thing, I just didn't get the thrill I used to get. I had some money put away and, since I was out on bond and doing the Supreme Court thing, I figured I had better start getting some shit together as far as being a regular person in society.

Downtown Sarasota, Florida, at the time, was trying to revitalize a building called the Kress Plaza on Main Street. I saw an opportunity to get involved in that.

I wanted to get into the fragrance, perfume, and soap business because I loved scents, especially when I smoked pot. They smelled even better when I was smoking. I opened a soap store in the old Kress building. I called it All My Soaps because, believe it or not, I loved the TV soap opera, "All My Children". I watched it all the time.

I based the look of the store on the opening scene with the leather-bound book that flips open. I had radio advertisements that were set up like a new episode of my store. A radio station, WDUV, in Sarasota played my ads, and they opened up with organ music and a woman saying, "And now, another episode of All My Soaps.'" It was like a soap saga for my store. Pretty fun and I thought it was creative. I enjoyed being an entrepreneur.

My driver, Bobby Zingg, had a girlfriend who talked about a coffee shop, which got me thinking about going into the coffee business as well. So I did. My coffee shop was called the Kress Coffee Exchange, and it was set up under a set of stairs at the Kress Plaza.

I was finally going legit. Two business ventures going and then I come up with another one. Down in the Keys, I had come up with an idea for a suntan oil applicator, and I was going to call it the SunBacker. I knew a guy in Detroit from the old days, Norm Lyle. He was a graphic designer, and I figured he could help me design the look and feel of the Sunbacker.

He came down to a beach house I was renting on Lower Matecumbe Key, below Islamorada in the Florida Keys. He stayed a week and we went swimming, sailing, fishing and designed the SunBacker.

I was motivated to make all these businesses happen before I had to go to prison, and before the Supreme Court came up with a decision, because now we had been granted certiorari and I was on my way to the United States Supreme Court. Although I still didn't get a decision until late '86 or '87, I knew I was going to get a date to go to prison.

They were going to issue a mandate for me to go, and it just became a matter of time.

Dennis and I moved to Colorado on Twin Sisters Ranch, between Nederland and Boulder. Beautiful country. My stores in Sarasota were doing well, my suntan oil company was getting ready to take off with the help of Norm's design skills and Dennis's investment, and I just needed to clean up my act, get my shit together. In fact, that suntan oil applicator actually made it into K-Mart stores in coastal regions for a test run, so things were going pretty good for me — as far as business. Personal vices, on the other hand, were still a problem.

Dennis and I were drinking considerably on and off. I had to put myself — I'm not going to tell you about all the times — in a couple of rehabs and dried out in the interim.

One time I went back north to Detroit and stayed for almost a year because I found a job to keep me busy and make a little extra cash. I worked at a American Jewelry & Loan, a pawn shop in Detroit, helping a guy named Les Gold put that together. He had a smaller pawn shop at a place called the Green Eight Center on Eight Mile Road, and then he moved it over to the old Northland Bowling Alley. That worked out for a while, but alcohol got in the way again, along with differences of opinion with Les about the store. I had a decent run there until I got drunk and fucked that up, too.

You know, I get mad and I make stupid decisions when I drink. I got an attitude over a situation that, when I look back, was not as serious as I thought it was in the moment. But, you know, I was an alcoholic and I decided to feel sorry for myself again. I thought everybody was against me, and that's what happens.

I continued to make bad decisions and the only common denominator in all of them (besides me) was the alcohol. A lot of my decisions were also tied to money, and you may sit there and say, "But the money is important."

No, it's not. Not that important.

It's better to live a life you're proud of—one that your friends and family can be proud of—than to have tons of money. If I can pull myself up by my bootstraps, anyone out there can do it too. Living a life full of goodness doesn't take money. It takes a conscious effort to make choices with others in mind. Selfishness and goodness don't live in harmony. Live for the greater entity or spirituality you believe in.

CHAPTER EIGHT

Angel

It's the late '80s now, and I'm waiting to go to the United States Supreme Court. I've been granted certiorari, which is a miracle because the United States Supreme Court usually hears 1 out of 1,300 cases. So remember that.

They decided to hear my case on rule 6B, which is two witnesses and the grand jury. The witnesses in my case were Randy James and Jerry Reinhardt. We called them Tweedle Dee and Tweedle Dum.

Two witnesses are not supposed to testify in the grand jury at the same time. That's been a law for 100 years. It's never gone to the Supreme Court, two witnesses in the grand jury, but I got there which was an honor, to be honest with you. I thought, *maybe I could win this and pull it out of the bag.* I don't want to spoil things for you, but that's not what happened.

Rehnquist and O'Connor wrote my decision and, while I'm waiting for my decision, I still partied and smuggled. Before the decision came through, I took Mishelle — who was an alcoholic herself —

out to Lake Tahoe and Heavenly Ski Resort and San Francisco. We're going to go spend some money because I've been doing a lot of business still, and Shelly Belly and I – we goofed off a little bit.

We rented a really beautiful place on Lake Tahoe where we spent some time and then found a casino to gamble. I won $9,000 at the roulette table my first night there at Harrah's. That was enough reason to celebrate for us.

I brought a bag of toot — cocaine — because I liked to snort it when I drank sometimes. I knew that I may be going to prison soon and I wanted to forget it all. I was good at masking my pain and depression with drugs and alcohol. I also was good at spending money like a maniac because, I thought, *Hell, I'm going to prison anyway.* It's not the right way to think, but that's how I dealt with it.

Mishelle and I had a lot of fun while we were out west. One night I had too much fun while I thought Mishelle was sleeping back in the room. We decided to take a shuttle from Tahoe to Reno and stay at the MGM Grand in the Presidential Suite. Mishelle thought that was a great idea. We really had a lot of fun gambling and drinking, of course. We walked up and down the streets, had drinks in different clubs, gambled in different casinos — it was a good day.

We went back to our suite and she was pretty drunk by this point. She said she was going to go up to our suite, but I wasn't ready yet so I told her I was going to play some more roulette.

Well, my old buddy, Johnny Boy, who happened to be Mishelle's ex-old man, had told me about the Mustang Ranch. Well, the Mustang Ranch is a brothel. At this time, there were two of them — the old branch and the new branch. I had plenty of money and I thought Mishelle went to bed and was passed out, so I tippy-toed away and went downstairs to "gamble," but that wasn't really where I was going.

Out the front door of the hotel I hopped in a cab and told the cabbie to take me to the famous Mustang Ranch. A lot of my smuggling buddies had all been there, most of them. Because that's what we did. We bought escorts from time to time.

I know I'm a pig. You can hate me, but this is the truth and I have to admit to some of the things I've done in order to continue healing. I didn't do a lot of good things, but the truth is important.

Anyhow, I went to the Mustang Ranch and stayed there for four or five hours. I went to the old branch and the new branch. When you were at the Ranch, you sat at a bar where you could order drinks. They had a little bell to ring and the girls would line up. If you didn't like them, you rang the bell and the next batch would come out. Well, I played that game until I was satisfied.

I went back to the MGM Grand and jumped into the elevator with these high roller guys who were also heading up to the same floor as I was. They wore cowboy hats, oversized belt buckles, diamond rings, horseshoe rings, you know typical high roller gambler, Las Vegas cowboys, kind of. But they had bucks. They had Rolex watches. I had my Rolex on, too, because I was a marijuana smuggler. I didn't look like a cowboy, that's for sure. Anyway, the elevator stops and we all turn left out of the elevator.

In front of us, all over the floor, is someone's belongings.

One of the Vegas Cowboys said, "Boy, somebody's in trouble."

Guess who was in trouble. Yep. It was me. These guys didn't know that was my stuff so I just said, "Yeah, me."

They said, "Oh boy," and they started laughing and slapped me on the back, those good old cowboys. I got to the door and I knocked because Mishelle had closed the safety latch on the door. The door only opens partially because she didn't remove the safety latch. She said, "What do you want?"

I said, "I wanna come in my room."

She said, "You're not coming in the room, I know where you were."

I said, "What are you talking about? I was out gambling."

She said, "I spoke to your taxi driver. I know right where you went. You went to that fucking Mustang Ranch."

Busted.

By now I know she's not going to let me in easily. She didn't know it, but in the room, I have a case where I had put my money. I had $10,000 or $15,000 extra cash. I have a special key to get into the case, though. I told her, I said, "Listen, Shelly, you've got to forgive me." Blah, blah, blah. I mean I was in that hallway begging for my ass for over an hour.

She finally decided that if I gave her $10,000, I could come into the room. I said, "Okay. Fine. I'll give you $10,000."

111

I did live up to this, believe it or not. I gave her $10,000. Mishelle was a little business woman. She's the girl we stuffed with money to do our dastardly deeds, hustling our money back and forth from Jamaica and the United States, all over the country actually.

That was Mishelle.

Let me say now, for the record, that Mishelle bought escorts in her life, too, so she was no goody two shoes either. People in glass houses can't throw stones. She let me back in for the money, and then we buddied up and went back to San Francisco.

I stopped back in Tahoe to pick up the rest of our things before we headed out for a tour of wine country.

While we were in Tahoe, I got a phone call informing me that I lost in the Supreme Court. It looked like I was going to prison. I got on a "live it up" type mentality because I'm about to be issued a mandate to go to prison so why not? Mishelle and I continued on to San Francisco and all through wine country where we loaded up on wine. I had it shipped back home.

After our trip out west, I went down to Florida to get my suntan oil applicator rolling and in stores. I had these stores up and running as a legitimate citizen. The businesses were helping me prepare, financially, to go to prison. But, you know, when you know you're going to go to prison, what do you do when you're an alcoholic?

Drink…of course.

My drinking has heavily increased now and I'm getting fat, too. To add to that, I'm also getting sad and ornery. I'm not the nicest guy to be around when I've been drinking, if you must know the truth. I get to Sarasota and I see an old friend, Dennis, my partner in SunBacker and we're going to start kicking that out.

I'm trying to put all these things together, because I'm waiting to be issued a mandate, right? The Supreme Court loss happened in February and I only had 90 days, maybe 4 months, to prepare.

I don't remember the exact time frame, but I had the opportunity to surrender myself because I've been out on bail. I didn't break my bond; I was a good boy. If, for some reason, I didn't turn myself in, I would lose a half million dollars in houses and money.

My mother's house was in there, too, for $100,000 or something. I can't have my mother kicked out of her house because of my antics. I was going to do the honorable thing and go to prison, which I did.

I got all my stuff together and prepared to go to jail. It was late summer, maybe early fall of 1986 when I surrendered myself, and I had to go get some extra mugshots in Tampa. Some friends took me and dropped me at Eglin Air Force Base in Ft. Walton Beach in the Florida panhandle. That's where I had to go to prison.

A former U.S. Air Force base, Eglin was where the Doolittle Raiders practiced their short take-offs in preparation for their famous "30 Seconds Over Tokyo." Now it's a Federal prison camp. It's no gold club like you may have heard, I can tell you that. Inmates at Eglin AFB didn't receive long sentences, and I was only in for 5 years — 15 at first, but I ended up doing 28 months, 17 days. I was all ready to do that, but not before I had a pretty big bender.

Dennis and I were living in our rented house in Colorado. We ate at a little diner called Sun Rise Cafe; we drank a lot and we were getting ready to do SunBacker. We even had girls sent to us from Tampa, Florida, actually.

I'm in the mountains of Colorado with my Rottweilers, my buddy, and I'm just trying to have a lot of fun before I head to prison, let me put it that way. I'm working between Colorado and Sarasota, getting all of my business affairs in order. I'm making arrangements with my SunBacker product, I'm pressured, and drinking my way through this. It comes time to surrender myself to Eglin Air Force Base, and my friends take me on that long ride.

First, we stopped and stayed in a Holiday Inn. Of course, I get a couple bottles of Chivas. I was drinking Royal Salute then. Dennis brought me some cocaine and a lot of marijuana. I mean, you know, I was numbing myself out good, because I knew I was going away for five years. And I was fat, out of shape, and drunk. Everything you can imagine. We partied and partied. And my friend — because I had some money stashed still — said, "Jerry, you don't got to go. You've got other IDs. You can just split."

I said, "Can't do that. Mother's going to lose her house. You know I can't do that." Not to mention my brother, Greg, who has cerebral palsy and is mentally disabled — I just couldn't do that to my family.

After a long night of partying, the next morning, they drove me up to Eglin Air Force Base. Now, you've got to remember. This is months of alcohol and snorting and getting ready to go to prison. So I had been pretty soaked with everything for months. I'm ready to check in at Eglin AFB with my minimal belongings. I had a gym bag with the things that I could bring. You know, there was a list of basics you could bring with you. I see the gate. They buzzed me so I could come in, and I went into the intake. The first thing they ask me is, "Have you had any drugs or alcohol in the past 24 hours?"

"Well, how about the past 24 years?," I said. "Actually, for the past couple weeks, I've been on a bender."

They're not going to let you go into the general population like that. I walked in drunk, and had been tooting cocaine. I looked like shit, honestly. They had to put me in a special area where I was going to dry out.

No medication, no doctors.

I think it was seven, ten days – I don't know – but it was a horrible experience. I felt like I was in Neverland, actually—sweating, puking, coming out all ends, you know, withdrawing.

I was in sad shape, moaning, crying, sweating, screaming, swearing. You know, I'm sure it was a wonderful sight to see. And I just had to grin and bear it.

After a time, I had pretty much sobered up, but I was still sick. The withdrawals were gone though. I dried out cold turkey. They didn't send a little doctor in to help you, they wanted us to feel the anguish and torment of that. Well, I sure as hell felt it.

I got to go out in the general population, so you've got to get your prison clothes now. At that time, you got blues and boots because you worked for the Air Force base.

My first set of clothing was too small. This is funnier than shit. All my clothes were too small. My pants came up above my ankles, the waistline was too tight, my top shirt was too small. I looked like fucking Baby Huey, okay? The boots weren't too small, though. They were too big. I was overweight and I looked ridiculous with the issued uniform.

It was pretty funny, and I know they were having a blast with it because I had to walk across the yard with my little bag of stuff to the area that I had to live. And everybody knows you're new, because they dressed me for the occasion. So I'm walking across the thing and, mind you, I had a few friends already there, and they knew I was coming, so they were expecting to see me. And they saw me, alright, and they busted out laughing at me, which I could take. I knew it looked pretty fucking funny, honestly. I mean, I was a sight — I was one hellluva sight, I'll admit that.

I went to the area where the cubicles are, where you're going to stay, and I had to go to the bathroom, because I'm so nervous, you see. And, I mean, I had to, you know, sit on the toilet. Well, I went to the bathroom because I still was probably having slight withdrawals, but I mean, things were coming out of me. At least I wasn't shaking anymore, just messed up. I had to get my bearings back on how to even think and walk, now that I was sober and I was going to be in prison for five years. It's kind of something I had to grasp, naturally, because I just lost my freedom.

Anyway, after I got done going to the bathroom, there was blood coming out of me. *Oh good, great! Now I'm bleeding out of my ass, and I'm in prison for five years.* I know God's talking to me here, believe me. He was kicking me around. I came back outside where my buddies were waiting for me.

Dig this, I come out the door and I see them all sitting on a ledge smoking cigarettes. As I walked over the threshold — and this seriously happened to me — a pelican shit on my head, and it ran down my forehead. They all saw it.

I wiped it off with my hand, and I said, "See how good this is? I'm coming to prison for five years, I'm shitting blood, and a pelican just shit on me. I obviously deserve this." You know, I had to laugh at the situation. I was laughing. We're all laughing. I'm wondering what's going to happen next because this was a hilarious start to my five years.

I decided, because I was in such bad shape, that one of the first things I was going to do was start working out and exercising. That's how I was going to bide my time. Now, I weighed 225 pounds when I walked into federal prison. Things were looking pretty grim at the time.

Pretty soon after I got there, I used the pay phone to call my mom and tell her that I was in prison. You had to wait in line, which was in the center, up by the control office at Eglin.

Hardy and Famer — we called them hacks — sat on the other side of the glass in control, and just watched everybody. There was a limit for how long you could talk, and then "the Hacks" made sure you got off the phone. You know, you'd see a lot of sad faces because they'd call home and nobody would answer. They're calling their wives, girlfriends, mothers and fathers. If you're doing time, pretty much plan on losing your old lady because the movie romance of "I'm going to wait for you," just ain't true.

One day my mother told me my Rottweiler, Charlie, was very sick, and he had something wrong with his intestines. She was taking him to the vet, and she would let me know later.

A few days later, I called back and she told me that Charlie's got all this cancer in him, and they want $2,800 to operate on him. His chances were, you know, 50/50. My mother knew where my money was — some money was buried in the backyard and some was up in the attic over the garage. I told my mother to get that money out and pay for Charlie.

I'm also waiting for a smuggle at this time that I had arranged just before I went into prison. So I figured, $2,800 to try to save my dog's life, that's a fair deal. Charlie did not end up making it through the operation. I had Charlie for 12 years – a long time. He was old.

Anyway, that was the end of Charlie.

When I first came in, the big news was that Aldo Gucci was going to prison at Eglin AFB. He had pleaded guilty to income tax evasion.

We also had Albert Nippon, who was the designer for Nancy and Ronald Reagan, for their inauguration. And we had Congressman Richard Kelly from the Abscam scandal, who was shoving the money into his pockets, and said he was doing his own investigation.

There were also a lot of Cubans and a bunch of black guys from D.C. — they were street dealers, and crack had just come out. I didn't even know what crack really was at this point, but it was popular. And, I mean, I was thinking, who wants to do a drug named crack? That was a joke amongst us older guys. So we had quite a cast of characters there in Ft. Walton Beach. Because D.C. is a federal area people had to go to federal prison for snatching purses, believe it or not.

Time's moving on and I'm adjusting. At night, the hacks walked by with their flashlights to do their nightly count. You know, they were always counting to make sure everybody's there.

Well, I got up one night, and I go in to the bathroom, and Aldo Gucci — a guy two cubes down from me — is there. He's washing his testicles in the sink, and I come in, and I say, "Aldo, Aldo, you know, I shave and brush my teeth there."

He said, "Oh, Chad" — he called me Chad, for some reason. I have no idea. This guy's, like, 80. You know, he's an Italian guy — really funny man. He worked in the laundry.

I'm still trying to tell him to stop it, and then he gets a thing with fish oil in it — cod liver oil…whatever…and then he's wiping that all over himself for his skin. It was a funny situation. I was razzing the old man, but at the same time, you know, I was being pretty honest.

I said, "Look, man, you're washing your balls in the sink, and you're making this place smell like fish. It's not that appetizing, Aldo." I used to go for walks with Aldo, and that was one of my favorite memories. I still don't know why he called me Chad. Aldo was a very good man.

Albert Nippon was a pretty nice guy too. They all signed a birthday card for my brother Greg, with all their names and prison numbers on it. I still have it today. Albert used to go into the cafeteria and Congressman Kelly would sit down and, you know, everybody knew that he said that he was doing his own investigation. That was part of his defense.

He didn't like me too much, I can say that, because I used to say, "You know, I was doing my own investigation too, in my airplane and they won't let me out either." He didn't like my sense of humor, but I couldn't help it.

Like, yeah right. I saw that footage of him putting that money in his jacket. They had the FBI agents dressed up as sheiks or Arab kings or princes or something. He got caught, bottom line.

I had quite an interesting time with those guys there, and I began to feel like I lived there. It wasn't so bad, because I was getting in extremely good shape. By this point, now, I can run 12 miles at a time, my weight dropped from 225 to 182, I could do 500 sit-ups, and bench press 300 pounds. This is the truth.

Actually, it saved my life, being in prison. Just like when I went to juvenile home in the beginning, when I was a kid, that saved my life too, as an incorrigible. These things have all been designed to save my life by you know who—Big Fats—upstairs. But there's no doubt about it. I just couldn't learn my lesson, so I had to keep getting punished, and, in a way, all my punishments turned out to be blessings. That's the point I want to get across for you.

Because I was the only one that had to go to prison in connection with the plane crash, I filed for what was called a Rule 35 or 36, whatever the hell it was. Actually, it was a reduction of sentence motion that I had my lawyer submit. It's called a 35-B. After my lawyer filed this, the system changed so you couldn't file a Rule 35-B anymore. I squeaked by just before you couldn't do it.

Now, Rule 35 at the time, was a joke. Everybody tried it, and everybody laughed when you were trying it, okay? Nice try, right? Just like your first time up for parole. You had "Do It All Paul," and "Maximum Maxine." Like, you think you're going to get paroled the first time you go up in front of these people? It's just a show. You're not going anywhere the first time.

I didn't even take my first parole hearing. I just didn't go, because I wasn't going to give them the satisfaction of turning me down. But I did file my 35-B, which cost a bunch of money. And everybody was joking.

I said, "Well, I'm waiting to hear about my 35-B reduction of sentence," and they'd go, "Oh, yeah, you better start packing. You'll be going home soon!"

One day I got a message to call my attorney. So I went up to the front. I used to watch everybody at those phones. They'd go up to the phone happy and then you'd see then come back from the phones very sad. We used to say, "Oh, there goes another lobotomy. He just got a lobotomy."

What happened to most of the guys was they would call their wives, and then their phone numbers ended up being disconnected. Happened to a lot of men. I watched it happen. I mean, I'm not making fun of them. I'm glad I didn't have that situation on the outside. I called my attorney and he said, "Are you ready?"

"Yeah, I'm ready."

He goes, "You're getting out, he granted it."

"Oh, shit," I said. I mean, I was like, *woah*.

Now, something you don't want to do is tell everybody in prison that you're getting out, because there could be some jealousy and soon things could be found in your area, things that can make you look bad because, as sick as it is, a lot of these characters — I say these characters because I'm not one of them — don't want you getting out because they know they're not getting out. I had to remember not to go running around looking happy and telling people that you got your phone call that you're getting out — especially Rule 35, because it didn't have a good reputation. Most people didn't get that granted. Well, I did, and I got it right before they took the rule away. I mean just before.

I'm happy but I'm trying not to act like I heard good news. I had to tell a couple of my friends, of course, because I had a lot of buddies in there. I had buddies in there from the Everglades; Pete Weeks and Keith Singletary. I also had made other friends there, but I just tried to keep my mouth shut. Somehow the information spread that I was getting out.

Now I had to get all this stuff together for halfway houses. Before I came to prison I had set up a smuggle with a boat that we still had called the Camelot. It' was a small sailboat. It was going to be a Jamaican trip, and Grubb and Ernest were going to go get it and sail it. Mishelle set up and rented a house over by Sanibel Island, and this smuggle — well, my mother was giving them money while I was in prison to keep things moving. I mean, we had to get supplies, make down payments on the pot.

Needless to say, Mishelle was on my visitor's list, and she brought another girl named Kelly, and I knew this thing was supposed to take place. She came to visit me, and guess what? Now I got my Rule 35B and my boat made it. Now God is rewarding me. I actually believe He was. You might not think God rewards you with something like that, but I did and I still do because I still had things to do in my life. I'm doing some of them right now as I'm sharing stories with you, whoever you may be. Things are going pretty good.

I was starting to feel very sad about my dog, and I had this Bunky who was a jerk. I wasn't a big fan of the guy. I said, "My dog died and I had him for 12 years."

He said, "So what?"

I said, "So what? You motherfucker..." I was going to go nuts on him, and he got scared so he went and told on me. They called me up and they decided to give me a piss test, and changed my number. First my number was 00171088A. Well they classified me to 00171088C. 'C' means that you have to be watched.

I got a new classification thanks to this little asshole, and then they decided to start piss testing me. When you get called up to go for a piss test, you better piss. You've only got so many hours to do it, or they're going to ship you to a lower level prison, a nastier one.

When somebody wants you to pee, you can't because you're nervous. They kept calling me to ask me if I could pee, and I was drinking gallons of water the whole day, but I couldn't pee because I was nervous. So you know, you have like retention.

It's getting down to the hour where they're going to do this, and I'm in a total panic, and I finally felt like I had to pee, but now I think I've got to shit, too. So I ran up to control and let them know I thought I could go to the bathroom. So the guy hands me this little tiny thing to pee in, but he has to come watch. You can't just go fill it, they've got to see you do it.

So he's got his little gloves on and he's going to stand over me, and I said, "You know, I'm not a girl but I'm going to have to sit down because there's going to be more than pee that comes out of me."

Anyway, I put that down in front of me and, at the same time, I blasted the bull. There must have been two months' worth in there because, boy, did I clean out from all that water. I gave the guy the little thing back, the little container for the urine and I said, "Boy, they must have to pay you a lot for this job." And he said, "None of it's worth it." He understood what I meant. I couldn't help but make a joke out of it, I mean, my God.

I had a counselor, Mr. Clark, and he didn't like me so he was disappointed that I wasn't going to be shipped because he knew I had a Rule 35. He was supposed to get me in the halfway house, but he didn't care for me or want me to get out of prison.

Believe it or not, most of them don't really want you to get out of prison. I mean, there were a few good guys in charge in there, but I'm going to tell you some of these guys that do this for a living, they're not that nice…period. And they like to see you suffer. It's not that it's your punishment, some of these sick bastards enjoy it, and I will say that as a fact of life, not my imagination.

Ok, the time is approaching to get ready for my halfway house.

I had gone for a walk one day and there was a dumpster over in an area, and I came around the corner there. There was a guy banging another guy and I was thinking, I've got to get out of here. You don't forget that sight when you go to bed at night, okay? Prison was getting on my nerves and I still didn't make it public knowledge that I was getting out.

The guys in my area knew though, and I could tell a lot of them didn't like that I was getting out. Mr. Clark was one of them. I used to have a connection to get porno mags, dirty magazines. I had them stashed around, and I used to pick out "girlfriends". I'd stick one up in the shower and I'd leave it there. He held these little town meetings for prisoners, and somebody told him I was doing it. He came in to give us all a lecture, and the whole time he stared at me.

He said, "There's some sick pervert in here sticking naked pictures of women on the shower stall walls. And you must be a really sick man to do that. If my boys ever did that, they would never hear the end of it!" He's talking about his kids.

Everybody's snickering underneath their breath because what do you think a man's supposed to do? I mean, you're in prison, that's not sick. I'm sorry, it's not. You want to see a female, believe me. I didn't want to see a guy. I saw plenty of hairy asses while I was there, I can guarantee you I wasn't attracted to any hairy asses, all right?

Mr. Clark called me on the intercom system to come to his office, and he sits back in his chair and he says to me, "Jerome, I've got some bad news. I put all your paperwork together to go to the halfway house, and I can't find it."

I knew he was full of shit and he was trying to pull my chain because if you show anything — any kind of anger or frustration — they can cut your halfway house off. I told him, "Well, you know, Mr. Clark, that's okay. I can only do 500 sit-ups right now so I'm going to work on being able to do 600. Really, I'm only going to get healthier while I'm here."

I mean, of course I was secretly very angry, but I cheered up, and I smiled at him, and thanked him for trying through my clenched teeth. Mr. Clark, wherever you are, remember me? That was mean, what you were doing to me, and I never made trouble in prison. You gathered comfort from watching men be sad, and I know that's not right.

I'm not saying everybody that works in prison does that, because there were some nice guys in charge of the show who really did care about people, but you've got some real sick bastards in there. I don't know where they are now, because this was back in the 80s. Maybe things have changed in the prison system, but I seriously doubt it. My papers were lost, which I didn't believe, and weeks go on and on and he finally tells me I can reapply.

So I did. I mean, what choice did I have?

It was a rainy day and I heard my name over the speaker to go to Mr. Clark's office again. As I'm walking across the yard where everyone hangs out, he comes walking out of his office area. He saw me and said he had more news on my halfway house, and when I had a chance, to come on in.

I was going to make the time so I went to his office. In the past he's teased me quite a bit and I don't know whether he's going to hurt me mentally again, but there is some news about my halfway house. It's hard not to get excited, get your hopes up, when you're thinking about getting out of the slammer, federal prison camp.

But this guy, he seemed to enjoy building you up, letting you down, building you up, letting you down. Psychologically screwing with you.

I went to his office, and he sat down again with that smirk on his face. He said, "You know what? I've got your paperwork. And do you know where it's been?"

He pulls up his ink pad. "It was here all the time."

So he purposely did this to me, and I wanted to snap on this guy right then and there, okay? But I thought to myself, No, no I'm not going to do that. I'm just really going to keep my cool and bide my time because I know my time is getting shorter.

He said he would contact me when I was going to be eligible since he has my paperwork back so it's a waiting game to see when I could go. Of course, Mr. Clark is taking his time with my halfway house now. He wanted to hang the bone in front of me. He wanted me to feel excited only to tell me he had no idea how long it will take now. All I knew for sure was he found my paperwork.

I was working a road gang where they'd take us in these big blue trucks with plywood sides and closed in. They were called RGs. I was on RG-10, so I worked for a guy named Mr. John Long. He was a citizen supervisor who had subcontracted to the government to take us, and our job was to work at the General's house, okay? And the General had a beautiful house on the base. We were going to clean up and re-sod his property. Basically, we were landscapers for the Air

Force base, but exclusively for the General. That was considered kind of a choice job. I learned how to lay sod really good. I learned how to take it up too.

His wife was a fox, and she used to like to lay out in the yard. Now he was on the water, but it was a very scummy, murky water. It was kind of a swampy backyard, but he had a beautiful home. His wife liked to sit outside with her women friends, and entice us. You know, when you smell perfume or you see a woman in a bathing suit and you've been in prison for a while…I'm going to tell you, your mind will wander.

It was kind of semi-torture but we actually liked it. We used these swing blades to clean out behind the swampy area. I had to get in the water with a swing blade, and I killed a couple of water moccasins with that. It was a nasty job, but if you didn't do it, you would have to go in the hole, and then get shipped to a worse prison. So we have a sod job for the General, and it quickly became obvious that John Long had been instructed to screw with me.

The General's property was huge and he wanted new sod because he had the St. Augustine garbage grass and wanted to replace it with fine Kentucky Bluegrass. But guess what? We laid every bit of that sod and his wife didn't like it, so what did we have to do? We had to pick all that sod up and put it back on the trucks.

It was torture, and when I made a remark about that to John Long, he moved me to another crew. I guess he and Mr. Clark had their own conspiracy going against me because John Long decided to put me on RG-2. The supervisor for RG-2 was a black man and he was known to take shit out on white people. This crew's task is to police the whole base with a plastic bag and a poker. Trash pickup all day. It's hot and you have to walk in your boots and blues all day.

I ended up becoming pretty friendly with this black crew leader, he was a civilian. We made buddies, and we started talking because he realized that I wasn't a racist, just a hippie pot smuggler.

It's unfortunate that certain people in our country feel negatively toward others just because they are different.

So we started making friends, and he would bring me burgers and stuff. John Long thought he was hurting me, but little did he know he wasn't, because I had a whole route that I could leave for the whole day.

Now Eglin Air Force was thousands of acres, okay? I had built a camp there, and I would go sit by the water and lay in the sun, just get lost in my thoughts. It was an escape for me. I had a watch, so I knew when it was time to go back to the area for the truck to pick us up. I had it pretty much made. I was living really well, to tell you the truth.

In the interim of my time in prison, a friend of mine who I had smuggled with had come to Eglin, and he was with Mishelle. Like I said, we all had the same girlfriends because that's the group we ran with. It was arranged for him to have a rendezvous with her, and he was on an RG crew that could go outside of the Air Force base. He arranged to have clothes because his crew was run by actual Air Force servicemen. They could be bribed, let's put it that way. A hundred dollar bill to those guys, living off of their salary and living on the base, was a lot of money. So we arranged for my buddy to go meet with Mishelle. Low and behold, Mishelle got pregnant, and her son, Nathan, is still my friend.

We managed to do a lot of things at Eglin Air Force Base when we could slide a bit of money under the table to the servicemen. We got guys out so they could go get laid, we got booze, although I never had a drink while I was there. I was completely dry. I didn't consider myself rehabbed at that time because it wasn't my choice to dry out. I was forced into it, so I didn't actually recover from alcoholism in any way, shape, or form. In fact, I was thinking about getting drunk as soon as I got out.

Alcoholics will never truly recover unless it was a conscious choice on their part to recover. You have to make the decision for yourself. I didn't make the decision when I went to Eglin, so I didn't recover.

CHAPTER NINE

Free Bird

The day had come for me to get out of prison and, unreal as it sounds, they didn't let me out until 12:01 a.m. — midnight. My friends had gathered at the gates to watch me leave. When I left prison, I got a cab, $100, a bus ticket and my papers because I was on my way to the halfway house. Technically, I was still in custody, okay…but I got my paperwork and I'm ready to be on the outside. It was raining, and there was a cab waiting to take me to the bus station in Ft. Walton Beach, and all my friends are standing out there on one side of the fence. I'm on the other side of the fence walking out, and as sick as it sounds, I almost wanted to stay.

Obviously I didn't want to stay that bad because I jumped in the cab.

When you're in federal custody you're not supposed to drink or do anything questionable, but I couldn't wait to get my hands on a drink. There's a liquor store right next to the bus station they take you to; it's practically connected to it. Before my bus was scheduled to leave,

I went and got some vodka and a six-pack of Budweiser, of course. I put that in my little carry-on, got on the bus, and settled in for a long ride.

It's 10 or 12 hours by bus to St. Pete and Tampa from Ft. Walton Beach. I figured I would chug a lug, then drink a lot of water so by the time I got back, I'd be sober. I also ate food whenever I had the opportunity.

When I got to the halfway house I would have to take a piss test and a breathalyzer test. Well, that all worked out and I pulled it off. That's not the point, though.

You see, through all that I went through, the first thing I did was get a bottle. My first action was to go straight for the booze. Bad thought process because, here I go again. I had some money saved, businesses rolling, and I was in better physical shape than when I went in. I had an opportunity right in front of me to make a better choice, but I just went and tore myself up again.

I had my soap store, my suntan oil applicator company, everything was pretty good. I had plenty of cash stashed because that sail boat smuggle that I had done while I was in prison worked out real good. Dennis and I got SunBacker — the suntan oil applicator that I invented with my old friend Norm Lyle — into retail, which was a big break for us. We found a way to help the disabled earn some money by assembling our applicators.

Norm had a connection with Barry Bremen, the Great Impostor. Bremen posed as a Major League Baseball umpire in the World Series, a player in a Major League Baseball All-Star Game, a player in a NBA All-Star Game, a referee in the NFL, and he played a round of golf in a Seniors Open. He even impersonated a Dallas Cowboys cheerleader!

At the 1985 Emmy Awards, he stood up, went to the stage and accepted the Emmy for Betty Thomas, an actress in the TV series, Hill Street Blues. Barry was a wild man.

Anyway, we worked on getting a deal with K-Mart up in Troy, Michigan. Barry and his partner Alan Harvith got us in with K-Mart. K-Mart ordered the product for their stores in southern coastal regions and in California.. Here was a big break for SunBacker.

While I was away, the soap store began failing because it had been pilfered through by people who were supposed to be watching it for me. There was barely any inventory when I got back, you know, the same old story. Out of sight, out of mind.

When I came back, I handled all that, but it didn't turn out well. The coffee shop was doing fine, and I sold it off to a girl I knew. The money I earned from the sale went to running SunBacker. So I was dumping a lot of bread — $80-90 Gs — into my invention.

I was putting money in but Dennis didn't have any cash left. I thought we should start a corporation, but Dennis' money was all over in Switzerland so he wanted to go and get it. I just wanted to go ahead and send the money and pay the taxes so it could come back to the United States. Dennis didn't want to do that, he was determined he was going to go over there and get it himself and bring it back.

Well, that turned out to be a bad idea. We've got all these pending orders and no money. I mean, I have no money. He calls me up to tell me he's leaving, and he gave me a time to pick him up in Tampa.

So everything is fine, I'm good. I know when he's supposed to be coming in, so I drive to Tampa. I had a Honda Accord LXI. I drove to Tampa and I'm thinking, *okay, now we've got the money to do the SunBacker.* He was going to bring the money in and we were going to live happily ever after, but that's not what happened.

I see Dennis waiting outside of the airport so I pull over for him to get in. He gets in the passenger side and pulls the door shut so hard that the window broke. I immediately knew things were not good.

"So, what's the matter?" I said.

Well, they caught him with the money in Atlanta, and naturally when you have that kind of cash — I mean, like, $75,000, $100,000, I don't know exactly — you're not allowed to just run around with that. You're supposed to declare it.

My worst nightmare came true. They didn't arrest him, but they did take all his information and the money. He was let go but we knew they could arrest him later, and they did. SunBacker went down the tubes because we had re-orders but I had nowhere to go to borrow the money. I'm not rich, I'm out of money. My mother didn't have a bunch of money, I had spent all of it. I drank and partied a lot of it away. I wasn't prepared for this moment, that's for sure. Alcohol got the best of me, again.

Dennis was eventually arrested, and he had to go to court. I guess he ended up pleading guilty and had to do a year or something in jail. When he got out, he naturally goes on a drinking binge. I'm still on one immediately after SunBacker tanked. I've been to half a dozen rehabs. I'm bouncing around drinking, depressed because I'm manic depressive too, and my whole ball of wax turned around again. I had the money from the smuggle I did, but I quickly went through that.

I went into rehab in Sarasota, a place called First Step. I started out on the right foot a little bit and went to work as a carpenter for some buddies of mine. I was pouring concrete and forming pool decks, getting back up on my feet again. I decided I was going to become a marine contractor, so I got my shit together and became a marine contractor in Sarasota and had a company called Dockmaster.

Now I'm dried out again. I straightened up enough so I could put myself back together, let's put it that way. I continuously did that for a while and I started making some really good money, and I got some good contracts. Things were going really well and I was going to the beach club on Siesta Key — Jay Foley owned that — a rocking place.

I rented an apartment on Avenida Milano and I was having a good time meeting girls. I'm in my late 30s, still pretty wild, in good shape, and feeling good because I have my own business again as a carpenter.

I go out to the beach club one night and I meet these girls. One of the girls looked good, I mean a really good looking girl. Her name was Barbie and, unbeknownst to me, Barbie owned an escort service called Sophisticated Lady. Not very good for Jerry. Her business partner was Bonita and they had a lot of young girls working for them. I eventually moved in with Barbie — I'm sure I don't need to tell you that this was a big mistake. She liked cocaine and alcohol, and the girls were, like I said, pretty young.

These girls made a lot of money around Sarasota. I didn't have to work as hard because Barbie wanted me around, so she gave me money all the time. I was just like, *this is pretty cool.*

Well, there's a price to pay when you live with a woman who owns an escort service, let me tell you, because I found out who the boss was, *and it wasn't me.* I was expected to do everything at her beck and call, and sometimes I didn't agree with that. Boy would she get mad! So I had to split from that girl. She chased me around Sarasota, and when she found out where I was living, she came over and just went nuts yelling at me. Someone called the police, and when they got there she told them that I was trying to strangle her.

Now, you know, I'm a felon, I'm still on parole, right. I had four, five years special parole and five years probation, so altogether I was going to be watched for a total of about eight years, which wasn't cool. I got in a lot of trouble for that incident with Barbie, but the police knew who she was and they got me out of there. One of the cops said, "Listen, you shouldn't be hanging around with that girl, man, because she's trouble." He was trying to look out for me. They knew who she was.

Anyway, I got away from Ms. Barbie, thank God, by the hair of my chinny-chin chin, because that girl was a whacko. She was taking Halcyon and all kinds of anti-psychotic things, and she was drinking like a fish and snorting cocaine all the time. She was a bad, bad, bad influence for people at the time. I'm sure she's a good person somewhere inside, because I believe everybody is, but I had a hard time finding the good within that girl, believe me.

I came back one night and she knew I was going to be leaving, and she was hiding behind the door with a baseball bat, and as I came into the bedroom, she took a full swing.

She was a tiny thing and didn't have much of a swing. Plus, I was strong enough that I put my hand up and caught that bat. She wanted to split my head open, then call the police and tell them I tried to kill her. I got out of that, too.

I'm telling you this lady was nuts. Very territorial, I guess the word would be. She thought I was one of hers, too. She didn't sell me to anybody as a male escort, but as far as she was concerned, she owned me. When she couldn't get her way she would scream that she could not take rejection.

Thank God I made it out of that situation, and I moved back out to Siesta Key. A young woman lived next door to me and one day I noticed a shorter guy with a newsboy style cap on at the charcoal grill. He had loaded it up with charcoal and then squirted lighter fluid on it before lighting it. Flames erupted out of the grill at first but they settled a bit.

The flames were still coming over the grate, but this guy went ahead and put the corn directly on the grill. Everyone knows — except this guy — that you don't do that. I didn't know who this guy was but I realized he needed some assistance. I walked out there and said, "Hey, man, you can't do it that way." I explained that he had to take the corn off the grill because he was going to get lighter fluid on it. I told him to rinse it off, wrap it in paper towel wet, and then wrap it in tin foil. You have to let the fire die out but the coals will continue to smolder.

Turned out that guy with the newsboy cap on was Brian Johnson, the lead vocalist for AC/DC.

I taught Brian Johnson how to do corn on the grill.

It was his daughter who was my neighbor, and he was visiting. He and his daughter came out to the beach club to hang out. They were both very nice to me. It was a fun experience.

I'm still a drunk, surprise, surprise, and I met a girl named Alicia, a little 21-year-old. I was hanging out with her and my marine construction company was falling to pieces because I was now on another major alcoholic binge. Let this be a lesson to anyone reading this: alcoholism and owning a business do not mix well. Needless to say, I had to put myself back in rehab.

Before I went to rehab, I went back to Barbie's to get some of my belongings. She was drunk of course, and that pissed her off so she smashed a glass on my bare foot. I was wearing flip-flops and it cut my foot pretty bad. I raced out of there as fast as I could. That lady was out of her mind. I drove back from Barbie's in Englewood to Sarasota, and went to the beach club to drink.

This was Memorial Day weekend in 1990. Well, my buddy, Brian LaPalm, is still bartending at the beach club. I could just walk in and have drinks — they made me really strong ones. I sat at the bar and told Brian what had happened. He knew who Barb was — he tried to warn me about her, but I didn't pay attention to him at the time.

So I'm getting drunker and drunker, and I decided I was just going to drive across the bridge to my mom's house. Brian told me not to go. I didn't listen, and I'm still on parole, too. I said, "I'll be okay." Well, I got in my car and went across the north bridge and, lo and behold, road block. There were cars behind me, cars in front of me, all lined up. It's a holiday weekend about 1:00 in the morning or close to it. I knew this wasn't going to end well.

I had a car phone at the time, wired into the car, and there was a little antenna on the roof. I sat in the car and I was pretty lit.

So I told my mother, "Listen, mom," I said "you don't have to do anything yet, but I'm going to get arrested in a few minutes."

My poor mother.

Mom was immediately worried, "What did you do Jerome?"

I said, "Don't worry, mom, you'll find out. I'll be going to jail."

I used to keep some money in a World Book Encyclopedia at my mother's house. I cut the center of the book out and I put it under "L" for loot. Before I hung up, I told her where to find the money. As I put the handset on the cradle, I leaned over and kind of fell over in the front seat. The Sarasota County Sheriffs, Sarasota City Police, and Florida State Troopers were all in on this combined effort to stop drunk drivers. What an asshole I was. I shouldn't have been out there drunk like that. I was lit to the max.

They asked me if I'd been drinking, and of course I said I had a few, even though I couldn't walk, could barely even talk. They attempted to give me the sobriety test. That did not turn out well. Plus, my foot was cut open from Barbie's big glass of scotch earlier in the day.

I wasn't in good shape.

I was failing every part of the field sobriety, trying to touch my nose and I'm still trying to talk these officers into just letting me go across the bridge and go home. I started to get kind of nasty and a couple of them started getting nasty with me.

I got in a fight with them.

Now, mind you, my judge had warned me that if I did anything, I was going back to prison. I hit a policeman in the face and they came down on me like every monster there was. I deserved it in my drunk-ass way. They had to do what they had to do, but I ended up in jail. I knew there were going to be some consequences for this because now I have to tell my parole officer that I got arrested. I had to stay in jail until I sobered up.

I was pretty drunk, and I refused to take a breathalyzer. They told me that if I refused I would get my license revoked immediately. I wouldn't blow for them, which means I lost my license. In the morning, my mother came, got me out. My truck had been impounded, which I had to pay to get out, of course. Since I pleaded not guilty I got my license reinstated. I drove back over to my mother's house and, naturally, sat down and got drunk. My mother…all she could do is shake her head. My poor mother.

I had to call Everett Springer, my parole officer.

"I got to tell you that I got arrested last night."

"Oh, I'm glad you called because I know that," he said.

I said, "Well, I didn't know if you knew it, but I had to call you and tell you, because I knew you'd find out, so there it is."

He goes, "Well, you're going to have to come in and see me, Jerome."

I figured I was going to get violated, you know. I told my mom I was going back to prison. My mother was very disappointed in me.

See, every time that shit pops up, when you're an alcoholic, you don't even give things like this the time of day. I'm on parole. I had good opportunities and here, after all this time, I'm punching out cops and getting arrested.

I mean, *what an asshole!*

Let's be realistic here. It's a good start to recovery to be able to call yourself an asshole, and genuinely mean it. Because you *are* an asshole. I go downtown to the federal building to see Everett. I go up the stairs, peering around corners expecting to see federal marshals or something. Everything is very quiet. Usually, if you're going to get violated and you're going to see your parole officer, that's when they snatch you and haul your ass back to prison. Right then and there.

I had what was called special parole. Special parole means you have to start every day of your time all over again, so all that time that I had involved in going to prison and being on probation was worthless. Before I left I told my mom I was going to leave to go back to prison. I said goodbye to her and even took a gym bag with the basics that I knew I could have with me.

When I got into Everett's office, nobody's around and then I heard this voice, "Come back here, Jerome." I'm creeping through this building because they didn't even have any secretaries there. It was eerie. I go back there, and Everett's got his feet up on his desk.

He said, "Sit down." I sat down and he continued, "What do we got here?"

"Well, we got me getting a little too drunk and the cops pissed me off, and I got in a fight with them."

He said, "Well, were you drinking?"

"Yeah, but they didn't need to get as rough with me," I said.

He basically cut me off and said, "Well, I'm not going to get in that with you today." He had my paperwork on his desk. "You know, you've been good now for some years. I have a lot of bigger fish to fry than you, and a lot of people do a lot worse than you do, but I'm supposed to tell the judge about this and you're supposed to go back to jail.

But I'll tell you what I'm going to do today." I mean, you can't tell me there's not a God. I watched a movie about Rocky Graziano starring Paul Newman, "Somebody Up There Likes Me". Well, somebody up there sure as hell likes me because this guy said to me, "I'm going to put this right here in my top drawer. I'm going to pretend this didn't happen. I don't ever want to see or hear from you about getting arrested or anything else here in Sarasota, Florida, or anywhere, or you will go back and start a five-year prison sentence all over again, Jerome. Is that understood?"

I said, "Yes, sir."

He told me to go, and I got up and left before he could change his mind. I mean, how fortunate is that? That is totally divine intervention as far as I'm concerned. All the stuff I'd been doing and this guy cuts me a break. That's a pretty fair, square deal. Walking out to my car, I couldn't help but jump in the air and click my heels together. I was a happy guy!

I go back to my mom's house and tell her what happened. My mother is just thrilled to pieces, but she said, "Jerry, when are you going to learn? This guy lets you go and you... you... are you going to do this anymore?"

I said, "No, mom, I don't think so." I couldn't really answer that sincerely because I still hadn't quit drinking in my mind yet. The first thing I did was celebrate my break, celebrate that my parole officer let me go. I got drunk at my mom's house like an idiot.

I have to run the gamut again for a while and I'm moving around, doing my thing and I have a girlfriend named Alicia now. I came home and she wasn't there.

I had a spaz attack. I was drunk and I smashed the whole inside of the house just because she wasn't there. She came home and cried and freaked out. She was a young girl. I didn't hurt her, just took off and went back over to my mom's house. I just had to leave town. I couldn't deal with it anymore.

My alcoholism was still just as bad.

See, you just keep going back to the drinking — the booze — every time and things will continue to crumble down on you. You think it's other people that are driving you to do this, but it's not. You're doing this yourself. I mean, it was all my fault. Nobody was deserting me. Everybody was trying to help me. I wasn't paying attention and, I mean, if you go through the past stories I've told you, you'll start to see the chances I blew.

If anybody's gotten second chances, I've gone way, way over my limit. I'm still getting good breaks, but the difference is now I see them and I take advantage because I know I have God on my side.

I decided I'm going to straighten up and get the hell out of town. I'm going to move back to Detroit and live with my friend, Norm Lyle. I'm going to reinvent myself and start fresh.

CHAPTER TEN

Seven Spanish Angels

I lived in Beverly Hills, Michigan for a period of time with Norm Lyle, only a mile or so from where I grew up. There was a house that I had been fixing in Southfield, off of 13 Mile Road, owned by the father of my friend, Jimmy Heidrich.

At that time I lived on Maryland in Birmingham with a woman named Amy. She was getting sick and tired of all my drinking, and was trying to find a way to get rid of me and my Akita, Benny.

I loved having Benny around because he could sense when I was going to have a seizure. I decided to go help take care of the Heidrich's rental property because, in a fit of despair, Jimmy had shot himself to death. He was homosexual and heavily into Codeine and opiates.

He was 38 years old.

Jimmy was always kind of depressed. He made a few suicide attempts before by, like, drinking bleach and he'd taken some overdoses of pills.

But he never succeeded until that night.

His parents earlier had put him up on 5 North at William Beaumont Hospital — the psychiatric ward. They released him after a while, but he slipped into depression easily. He came over to his parents' house and he had told them that he couldn't sleep.

After his mother offered him some hot cocoa, they all went to bed.

When they woke up, Jimmy was gone. They just thought he went back to the house in Southfield. Mrs. Heidrich drove over to his house and walked through the front door. For a moment, she thought he wasn't home, but she noticed his coat on the floor in the living room. Jimmy was nowhere to be found. She turned around and stumbled over him. He had taken his father's .357 Magnum and blown his brains out.

Here's depression, suicide, and drugs again, okay? Do you want to be a substance abuser? You don't, really. You may think it's fun and you won't become addicted, but you will. And you can't get out of it unless you make some serious changes in your life and ways.

Jimmy's dad, Larry Heidrich, was an old millionaire. Amy had thrown me out of the house on a Sunday morning. I didn't really have anywhere to go, but Mr. Heidrich offered me a job to put the house back together because Jimmy had taken it apart out of sheer depression before he killed himself.

The kitchen was totally ripped out, down to the wall studs. He took the stairs out. He took the bathroom out. He took the drywall out. He stripped the inside of the house before he popped himself.

Anyhow, Mr. Heidrich said that I could stay at the house while I worked. Remember, I had acquired some carpentry skills from my experiences in Florida.

Well, I turned that into my living in the 90s so this was a good job for me. Since I had Amy's place to stay originally, I told Mr. Heidrich that I didn't need to live in his house. However, when Amy kicked me out, I needed a place to stay. I jumped in my Volkswagen van after I loaded up my belongings and my Akita, Benny.

It was ice cold outside, but I had on flip flops and a pair of shorts. I was just heading straight over to the Heidrich's place. I was already lit on a Sunday morning.

Volkswagen engines have a tendency to blow, but they were small so you could just pop another one in the back. Well, it happened to me that Sunday morning right in front of the old church I had attended as a kid. I hadn't been there in twenty years since my confirmation and my old man's funeral. I needed to call for help so I walked into Ascension Lutheran Church.

Services had just let out and the parishioners were having donuts and coffee after church, and here I come stumbling in with my broken down van out front; shorts, flip flops and I'm toasted.

This is where God steps in. As I said, I don't believe in coincidences.

I see some of the same ushers that used to know my father—old men now, though. They were still ushers for the church. Now I was in my 40s and I didn't think they'd remember me after a few decades, but they did.

I approached them and told them who I was, told them my problem, and they went to work right away. They helped me get a tow truck, gave me a ride to the house I was going to with all of my clothes and everything.

I see God at work that whole morning.

I was so drunk and shouldn't have been behind the wheel and my engine blew right in front of a church – God's house – and not just any church. The church where I knew people once upon a time and you know what? They welcomed me and helped me without a second thought. Think that's a coincidence? I don't believe so. I believe these are acts of God. You may think I'm crazy, but there are so many instances when I felt God's presence, felt his intervention in my life. It took me many years to realize that was what happened.

So, anyway…this is the house I'm going to work on. The Heidrich house where poor Jimmy killed himself. I mean, all this happened just before I got thrown out by Amy. My dog Benny was coming with me. Now, remember, I just got the boot from my last place because I was drinking too much. So when I got to the Heidrich house, I didn't have to worry, so I brought a bottle of rum with me.

But something happened that made my hair stand up on end.

Part of the agreement was that I would not just complete the construction projects but I would also clean up where Jimmy died.

There was dried blood in an outline of his head from where he died and it congealed. Benny laid near that spot – don't ask me why. I laid down in the bedroom, but there were no walls at this point, just framing. So I could see through the studs, you know, the skeleton.

It's about 1:00 a.m. and I turn the lights off. Just as I was dozing off, Benny started howling like a wolf. I mean, I got the willies. My nerves were rattling so, naturally, I opened that bottle of rum and got drunk off my ass. I was freaked out. I will never forget that Benny had picked that specific spot to lay down and then he suddenly sat up and howled. I mean, I believe in this stuff, right? I believe Benny saw something that maybe only dogs can see. I don't know, but something set him off. Something about that particular spot and that particular moment. You may think I'm nuts, or maybe that I was just drunk but I'm telling you something happened that night.

One of the renovations in this house was with the stairway. Jimmy had previously taken out the stairs that led to his studio. A talented artist, he created beautiful stained glass and painted a lot of different things. I put in attic stairs instead and just closed off the regular stairs since it was an attic-type space.

I had to renovate that attic space and remove all of Jimmy's art supplies and work. Well, I'm filing through all his art shit, and I come across this painting — this is no shit — the same fucking bloody imprint that was in the wooden floor where he died. It was painted in red, and it was titled "Final Solution".

What the fuck was this?! It looked like the shape of Jimmy's head, I swear to God. At this point, I'm spooked beyond measure. He had painted this picture, according to his brother Glen, quite a long time before that. But it did resemble, like…I would say 99% of the imprint that was on the floor where he shot himself and died. Whatever precognition or whatever was going through his artsy hands, it was stained into that floor, and it remained there the whole time I worked on that house. The second I finished working at that house, I got the hell out of there.

I moved in with another friend of mine named Rick Mott. I started hanging out there and continued working as a carpenter. While I was there, I went driving to go to the store and I enjoyed cutting through neighborhoods, the suburbs, just for the hell of it. I'm going down this one street, and I look to my left, and I see this guy that looks really familiar to me.

I stop, and I realize it's my old friend, Bill Whitney.

I stopped, and I said, "Willy!" and he said, "Lill!" So I got out of the car and we're talking. He said, "You don't mind if I have a cocktail, do you?" I was not surprised by this statement because Bill was a heavy drinker. I hadn't seen him for many years—it had been probably close to 15 years, because the last time I saw him was for the 1984 World Series when I came up from Florida and he and Norm Lyle and I went to see the Detroit Tigers beat the San Diego Padres. Now we're way into the '90s and I see him this day.

I drive over to his house and Willy's already drinking. It's morning. I was kind of getting on a sobriety thing, right, but I could tell he sure wasn't. He was living with some girl named Joanne, who was a major alcoholic, and they were having their cocktails in the morning.

It's just what we alcoholics do.

When you're a serious alcoholic, you start getting shaky if you haven't had a drink after about 4 hours. That's all it takes to start getting the DTs. Anybody out there who reads this knows what I'm talking about. You need that drink; it's not just your imagination. Your body goes through fucking withdrawals quick. Okay? I mean, you start feeling real crummy, shaky, jittery, nervous — you really don't know what to do. Willy was getting to this point. He offered me a drink but I declined. I'm just there to sit with him and bullshit.

We decided, hell, we're going to start hanging together. I knew Whitney needed to get sober, and I wanted to help him out. I wasn't going down the tubes. Things were going well for me. I had a nice van then, a lot of tools. I was on a "Jerry Straight-Up," which I'd go through now and then.

But every time I fell, I fell further and further down the alcoholism black hole.

Believe me. Alcohol is a progressive disease.

It gets worse. It doesn't get better. If you keep feeding it, you're going to get sicker and sicker and more addicted as time goes. It's the same thing with pills because by the time I ended my career in drinking— look, you've got to understand; I'm eating Vicodins, morphine, Ativan, smoking pot, and drinking at least a liter of vodka a day — if not more — plus beer and wine. I mean, I can't really explain to you what a major alcoholic I was.

139

But I'm not an alcoholic anymore.

I don't even consider myself a "recovering" alcoholic.

I'm a *former alcoholic.*

I prefer to say it that way. I know there's some that don't agree with that, but you're not going to catch my ass drinking again. I can tell you that. It's a road to nowhere.

Everyone loves a drinking buddy, right? Well, now I got Whitney and I'm about to fall off the bandwagon big time. Willy decided he needed a new drinking buddy and, of course, I needed one.

He was tired of drinking with Joanne. She was a lunatic alcoholic—schizophrenic, bad teeth, everything was wrong with this poor girl. She was starting to have liver problems and the timing for Whitney to leave was perfect.

Whitney and I had reunited. Let's put it that way. So we were on a good week-long binge or so, and we had just picked up another liter. When you're drinking like we were drinking, a couple liters of vodka in a day for two full-blown alcoholics is not that much.

Believe me.

I mean, it's a lot, and you're drunk, but it's nothing for you to go through that kind of alcohol in a period of part of a day, especially when two of you are sucking on it. We weren't even mixing it, just drinking right out of the jug.

We drove over to his sister Jan's house and ended up sitting in the driveway. We didn't even want to drive anywhere else because of our drunkenness. So we were just parked there and sucking down the booze, listening to rock and roll and intoxicating ourselves to the maximum.

We talked about all the shouldas, couldas, and wouldas. We had all the answers to solve the world's problems with that juice in us.

As we're talking, Bill went into a complete alcoholic seizure. Seizures don't just happen when you're quitting drinking, but also if you drink too much. Okay?

There's a dog house in the front of these cargo vans, and he somehow got himself so trapped and wound around in there, that I couldn't get him out. His eyes were rolling back in his head, he's foaming at the mouth, and then just went limp.

I can't get him out of this dog house and his sister was in the house. So I went in and told Jan that Bill just had a seizure, and I thought we needed to call an ambulance.

"He needs to go to the hospital," I said.

She said, "Well, do you really think so?"

I said, "Listen" — I was drunk and not sure she believed me at first—"I'm telling you we gotta get him to the hospital." Eventually she called 9-1-1 and the ambulance came. They had to take the dog house off and all kinds of stuff to get poor Willy out of there.

He was rushed to the hospital. His blood alcohol turned out to be over .5! That's bad. He was admitted into Providence Hospital in Southfield. That hospital actually specialized in alcohol abuse and side effects. I didn't know that at that time. We both went to rehab after this, but needless to say, Willy had to spend the night because they were going to dry him out. I slept on Jan's couch while he was in the hospital.

The next day, Jan and I went to go see Bill. He was having the tremors and was a little delirious. They were loading him up with Ativan. He looked like an 80-year-old man, to be honest with you. His mouth and whole face shook when he tried to talk. Of course, he didn't really even know we were there. Delirium from alcohol withdrawal is terrible to watch. You know you shit yourself? Did you know that? I still didn't learn from this experience. Exactly how much is it going to take for me to learn? If you're doing any of this shit, I hope you learn before I did. That's why I'm doing this. I'm spending my own money to do this, so you better fucking listen.

Jan and I leave the hospital and she's driving. We pull up to the streetlight at Greenfield Road where Providence Hospital is, and there's a car eeking up. I'm drunk. Remember that. I'm still drunk. I should've been in the hospital, too, because my blood alcohol was way out of line.

Jan pulls into the left turn lane at the light, and there's another car turning left from the other direction. The other driver gives Jan the signal to turn. She starts to turn left and here comes a Cadillac through the light.

Bam! T-boned on the passenger side — my side — and the car rolls. It was another major accident.

The ambulances showed up and, you know, Providence is right there so they didn't have to come from far. I'm in the front seat when the cops get there, and the car's T-boned, rolled over. Someone is trying to get me out of the car, and a cop keeps asking me, "Did you have your seat belt on? Did you have your seat belt on?"

And I said, "Yes, but I took it off."

Incidentally, I didn't have my seat belt on in the other rollover accident in New York either. Do seat belts save lives? I don't know. I think not having mine saved me a couple times. I didn't have one on when I crashed my airplane either, by the way. What can I tell you, I'm stupid. So, there.

Anyhow, I didn't want to go to the hospital, but the cops smelled alcohol on me and said I was going to go to the hospital or I was going to be arrested.

I said, "What?"

She said, "You've been drinking."

And I said, "Yeah, but I didn't do anything wrong, I'm not driving the car."

This was my logic. Anyway, I don't know if she could've really done anything, but I got in the ambulance and went to the hospital. They checked me out and everything and you know where I ended up?

In the room talking to Bill Whitney.

If this isn't divine intervention, tell me, tell me right now, what else could it possibly be?

Whitney dried out and we decided we're going to go into rehab together. Here's another show called "Bill and Jerry Go to Rehab." We ended up in a 30-day rehab and we're going to dry out and live happily ever after.

Whit stuck with it and he's sober today. For me? It didn't stick.

We did the rehab, we dry out, we do the 30 days. I picked us up some jobs working for a guy named Howard Sikora and his wife — both alcoholics. You don't know how many there are out there, my friend. Alcoholics are everywhere — they live in the suburbs; they're rich, poor, have kids, married, single — they're all around.

After I got out of rehab I found another house to help work on in Detroit near Seven Mile and Telegraph Road, kind of in the 'hood. But my back really started to hurt and I had to be in a wheelchair for a while so, you know, I wasn't doing all that well.

Bill was still working for Sikora, but I was sitting around the house with my dog, Benny. One particular morning stands out in my mind. I was sucked in to the breaking news happening — 9/11.

I couldn't take my eyes off of it, like all Americans. It was heartbreaking, unnerving, terrifying, and just downright upsetting.

You know when an alcoholic sees something sad on TV, you know what they do, don't you? They have a drink because, oh my God, it's all they can think of to do. I was actually watching the regularly scheduled morning news when the first plane hit. Of course the anchors cut to the breaking news and, like most Americans that morning, I watched the second plane hit on live television.

Well, back on the bottle, of course. That's what we do.

As alcoholics, we find any excuse to have a drink. Good news: drink in celebration. Bad news: drink in sympathy. It's Friday: drink because it's the weekend. The sun came out: drink because it makes you happy. It rained during a BBQ: drink because you're bummed.

It doesn't matter, you think you need it. You'll use whatever situation comes across to justify your desire and to get your hit. Whatever your drug of choice is, you know you're going to do that. And that's a bunch of shit. You don't need to do that.

I've come to realize that it's very hard for those around you, who love you, to just sit back and watch you. Everybody thinks maybe they're going to be the person who saves you.

The reality is nobody else is going to save you but yourself.

You're going to have to save your own ass.

There is a catch to that, actually, because God's trying to save you the whole time. He keeps sending you messages and you keep blowing it, but eventually He's not going to give you all those choices. You've got to understand that. You're going to run out of chances, run out of time.

Now, for whatever reason, I have been fortunate, because like I always say, I didn't go find God, God found me. I went through a lifetime of this bullshit because I didn't listen the first or second time. Or third or fourth, really. I now know that I endured so I could share a bit of wisdom that I attained the hard way. Sure, people tried to help me, but I didn't listen.

That doesn't mean *you* don't have to listen. You should pay attention to me. Maybe God is talking through me, I don't know. I do know that the life I led did not bring happiness or joy. I didn't feel love. I know all about the shit some people can go through. Hell, I went through some of it. It's hard and it hurts, but turning to alcohol or drugs is only going to numb the pain temporarily. Eventually, it comes back in a stronger torrent.

You can win. *You can beat this.*

You matter and you deserve to beat this shit. I want to give you a boost. That's all I can do for you. I can give you a boost and you better believe I'm praying for every lost soul every day.

I had another big job for a very rich guy and his wife in Rochester Hills, Michigan — the Desereses. Dave and Liz Deserese were super nice people. They had a company that prints all the stamps that the United States government buys, so they ran 24-7.

You don't think there would be a lot of money in that, but there is. You think about all the stamps that are used across this country, and they supplied a good part of it.

They were wealthy, to say the least. They were also very nice people, and I had been working for another company called Midwest Builders subcontracting jobs. I was getting into basements, carpentry work, some fancy stuff.

I did a job for a guy named Mr. Fudge who was buddies with Dave Deserese. I was with Amy at the time — she was the one who kicked me out and I found myself fixing up the Heidrich's house.

Well, she and I had moved out to Farmington Hills to an old farmhouse. It was a pretty cool place and I was doing my side gig carpenter stuff and we had Benny. Life was good for the moment. Good with the exception of my drinking.

Amy was getting very upset with my alcoholism, which she had before many times, but she gave me chance after chance because there's something about women that makes them think they can help us. We're going to change for them. Each woman I've been with has thought that; I'm not making fun of them but they all thought they could be the one that makes the difference.

In reality, the only one who is going to make the difference, like I've said before, is you. Because if you don't do it, there is nobody in this world that is going to do it for you. I'm sure there's the rare "But I fell in love," or "I met this girl who changed me" stories.

That is not typical.

It's extremely rare for an alcoholic to stop drinking for someone other than themselves. It's usually you and God. God is involved in your life the whole time. Because if not for Him and His grace, I would be a dead man. There's no doubt about it.

I came home one night after drinking a lot. I was making good money because the Desereses were paying me top dollar and I was doing a really nice job on their basement. I was slipping into my heavy drinking again though. It seems like every time I start making decent money, I start drinking more and more.

I'll say it again: Alcoholism is a progressive disease; drug addiction is a progressive disease. That's real talk. It progresses, worsens, destroys. It will tear you and those around you down. Your life does have a purpose, you don't have to sit in the corner and be a crybaby and say nobody loves you, because it's exactly the opposite.

People can't stand to sit there and watch you destroy yourself. You can't self medicate because that leads to a dead end. The only substance that should be used for healing and medical reasons is marijuana. You don't have to smoke it; the oils are good, too. There are great medicinal benefits and studies are proving that.

I went to prison for pot, remember that. Smashed an airplane, got arrested and got in a lot of trouble a bunch of times over marijuana, and I'm still behind it. It's the only drug I used that I never did bizarre behavior with. I never got depressed with marijuana. The cannabis helped me, so I can't knock that. The alcohol and the other drugs though, I will definitely knock, adamantly.

I don't really know exactly which time this was, but Amy had decided enough was enough. I was working for the Desereses and getting tired of that job; I had just about finished it. I worked with a crew — a big, biker guy named Big Mikey, who had long hair and resembled a jolly Santa Claus. He was a boozer, too, and another buddy, Tony — who was earning about $800 a week. I took in, like, $1,600-1,700 a week. We made serious money working for the Desereses.

Amy was happy because Amy liked money. Sometimes people will look past some of the negatives, even if you're a drug addict or alcoholic, if you give them money. Most people won't admit that, but it's a fact. I watched it happen time and time again. Well, eventually they'll get fed up.

I came home from work with Mikey and walked into the back door of my house, and it was super clean. I went through the kitchen and into the dining room. Those rooms were super clean too.

You know what? Amy ditched.

All the furniture was gone—everything. Tables, chairs, lamps… *everything*. There was a little office off to the right by the bathroom, and there was one single bed in there with a little TV and telephone. A landline. That was going to be my room because she was gone.

I got nervous, and I had to take a shit, so I went into the bathroom. You know what else she took?

The damn toilet paper. The huge Costco super gonzo packs.

I'll admit that my drinking was getting out of hand, and she couldn't take it. She tried hard, I'll give her that; she was a good girl, tried to be a friend to me. *But all the fucking toilet paper?*

I'm sitting on the toilet and I yell to Mikey to go to the store and pick up my quart of rum for the evening, some Coca-Cola and some cigarettes. And toilet paper.

When Mikey returned I proceeded to get drunk, because an alcoholic finds an excuse to drink no matter what happens. My old lady left me and I don't have shit in the house. I'm going to drink for that.

So I'm getting a buzz on and the house is empty, and I'm using some choice words because my shit is gone and I'm pretty pissed. The furnishings, frying pans, dishes — the house was clean, I'll say that much.

My phone rings, and it's a lady but I can't really understand her that well. She said, "Are you a carpenter?"

I said, "Yes ma'am."

You've got to remember I've just run out of work and Amy just left me all in the same day. I'm ready to hit the bottle hard. I also believe that I have the right to do that because, again, I'm feeling sorry for myself. I just got fucked over, didn't I?

Not. I fucked myself over. Nobody's fucking you over, you're fucking yourself, okay? I said, "Yes ma'am, I am a carpenter. My name's Jerry."

She said, "Well, I have your card here. I got it at my hardware on Evergreen and Eight Mile."

I said, "Really, I didn't know I put a card there, but I might have dropped it off when I was buying paint or something, nails, who knows?"

Evidently she picked up my card while she was at the hardware store. She tells me that she needed a reliable carpenter, somebody who's honest because she was blind. I said, "Okay, well, I'm not going to rip you off, but how are you calling me if you got my card at a hardware and you're blind? How did you dial me?

She said, "My grandson helped me dial your number."

Now, I don't know anybody at this hardware, so then again, Margaret Jackanin — this lady — what a great influence in my life. She is part of why I'm still alive. She was put in my path by someone and do you want to guess who it is?

My big fat buddy...God.

God told Margaret to call me at this precise moment because I was on my way to a major binge. I had all the excuses ready to go, okay? My girlfriend left me, I was done with my job, the furniture was gone, I had no toilet paper for crying out loud. Now isn't that a perfect opportunity to feel sorry for your own little ass? Instead, here comes God and He had a blind lady call me who picked my card up at a hardware store and I have no idea how it got there.

It's two days before Christmas and I told Margaret that we'd be over the next morning — Christmas Eve morning. I asked Mikey if he was going to be able to make it, and he said he would be there. I told her we would be there early in the morning about 8:00 or 9:00. She passed the phone to her grandson, Darrell Henning, and he gave me the directions and address.

When I hung up the phone, Mikey and I turned to each other and high-fived because here we got another job out of the blue. Something greater than all of us was at play here. Call it your higher power, God, whatever you want to call it, but "Big Fats" intervened to save me again.

The next morning I'm just pacing the floor because I'm worried Mikey isn't going to show up. He pulled through and we drove over there, introduced ourselves, and she started showing me all the projects she wanted done. I explained my rate and that I charged by the hour and materials.

147

Margaret was in her late seventies and, though legally blind, she had some peripheral vision. I started working the very next day. I'm feeling positive and I want to keep my shit together because I have a job. I mean, I can't be a total drunk on a job and use power tools, you understand that.

Margaret had another house that she asked me to begin working on. She allowed me to live in that house while I fixed it up and also did the other projects in the home she lived in. It was a great break for me, and Margaret played a big role in my life during that time both emotionally and spiritually. I'll never forget her.

She had asked me to fix a deck and I needed to pick up materials to get started so I headed over to get the money to buy what I needed.

Well, when I got there Margaret was dead in her chair.

Her grandson was already there and all he could say was, "She's gone."

It was the end for me, too, in a sense. It's like a winding mountain road with switchback after switchback. That was my life. At times I'm heading in the wrong direction and someone or something happens in my life and I make a switchback toward picking myself back up. I cruise along and then I come to another switchback and I'm moving in the wrong direction again. That was my life — switchback, switchback, switchback. But now, I see that I was still climbing. God was there with me guiding me up that mountain even though I made many poor choices. After Margaret passed away, work dried up for a bit and I was back on another drunken binge.

I eventually found a new place to stay in a nicer part of Royal Oak. I rented the bottom part of this house from a guy named Rick who happened to be a crackhead. One day I heard a knock on the door, so I answered the door with a 40-ounce bottle of beer, no shirt or shoes. I'm a friendly guy, right. There's a guy standing on the stoop and he says, "You Jerry, the carpenter?"

I said, "Yeah."

He goes, "Well, I've got a garage I need some work done on. I live right down the street here, and I heard maybe you could do that. I saw your truck so I stopped."

The words 'Cross Country Carpentry' was on the side of my van. I said, "Yeah. Sure, man, I'll come and look at it."

I stepped through the door, and before I could say anything, there were Royal Oak Police on me with automatic weapons, flak jackets, hiding behind cars. I literally — this is the truth — shit my pants.

They yelled, "Freeze! Freeze!" They said I was being arrested for felonious arson. I'm thinking, *felonious arson? What the fuck?*

Excuse my language.

Dig this, man. I was taken into custody, and I'm in the car with the Royal Oak cops, and they asked me what I lit on fire.

I said, "Fuck, I don't know." See? That word gets the point across.

I was confused, and I need to get the point across to these cops that I have no idea what they're talking about. They're asking me questions about this fire, and the only fire I can think of would be when I had a fight with Amy, my ex-old lady, and the bottom of a curtain got lit with the lighter. I threatened to burn her house down during a fight.

I was, of course, drunk at the time. I told the cops that I put it out and nothing ever happened. That happened, like, six or eight months ago. That cop said, "You're telling me that I'm picking you up for lighting a curtain on fire that didn't even burn anything?"

I said, "That's the only fire I know about, sir."

I just want to get out of this car because I'm pissed that I'm getting picked up for felony arson. You can imagine that I wasn't very comfortable, with my pants full of crap.

I know some of these stories get a little gross for people, but I have to tell them to you the way they happened. This is real life.

Anyhow, they take me to Farmington Hills, because that's where this crime was committed.

Now O.J. Simpson is on trial at this time. Domestic violence is a very hot topic during this period and I fell right into the middle of it with this curtain fire thing. I have to be arraigned in front of a judge in Farmington and the prosecutor is a female who is all about bringing the guys down, okay? Keep in mind that I have all these felonies from smuggling marijuana, so they wouldn't give me a bond because they said I was a flight risk and a dangerous man…of course.

This was a time in our nation that had a bright spotlight on anything to do with domestic violence. Protesters were marching out in front of the Oakland County Courthouse in hopes of making more headway on domestic violence offenses, and I was a timely target.

Things progressed, and I have no bond. I'm basically screwed because I don't have the money I used to have and I can't get a lawyer. Amy, my dear friend, had done this because they came to investigate me at one point, and she told them I was going to come and get my tools once, which was a long time before.

She happened to mention that I lit the curtain on fire when I was drunk. A female detective said, "Oh, that's felonious arson," and that's how the charge came down the pipe.

The burn on the curtain was, at the most, a quarter of an inch, to be honest with you. That was the evidence they were bringing to court to try me.

Well, they kept me in that jail for over six months and continued to offer me deals of 5 to 10, 8 to 12.

I said, "No, no, no. I'm not going to do that. I'm going to have my day in court!"

I could not believe in my mind, you know, that this was going to end poorly for me. I'd been on trial for a long time previously in connection with the DC-6 plane crash. They had a lot more evidence than a little piece of curtain. They had, like, 26,000 times the amount of evidence.

They continued to offer me deals. I continued to turn them down. Finally, they brought me a deal that allowed me to get time already served and five years probation if I plead guilty for arson. I'm not doing that. I'm not an arsonist.

I said, "I want to have a trial." Summer has long passed and we're into winter in Michigan and I'm still sitting in jail over this bogus charge. The snow was falling and it was actually pretty peaceful. Fresh snow has a quietness to it that makes you feel hopeful, almost warm in a strange way. Maybe that's why it's often called a blanket of snow.

Someone came to get me at about 5:00 p.m. and said, "Mr. Lill, come on, get up. You're going to trial." I knew for a fact that I wasn't going to trial that late in the evening, but I got up anyway. I put on my civilian clothes and went to the court of an old judge — can't remember his name. Of course the prosecutor is present, and so is my public defender. The judge reads off my name and he said, "So, Mr. Lill, I see here that you were a little drunk when this took place."

I said, "Oh yeah, no doubt about it."

He said, "And you've been in jail now for six months."

I said, "Yes, sir." He's wearing glasses and he lowers his chin to look over the top of them directly at the prosecutor and he asks, "So, why has Mr. Lill been in jail for six months for this?"

She said, "Well, your honor, he's a convicted felon and he is a flight risk, and due to the seriousness of the arson, I believe that Mr. Lill should not be out. He's a danger to society."

The judge says to her, "Mr. Lill is not an arsonist. Sounds like Mr. Lill's got a problem with alcohol to me, but I don't see anything here showing he committed arson. If he did…" He was cut off by the prosecution and she said, "He's committed at least a misdemeanor."

He said, "Then he's already done three times the sentence for a misdemeanor. I don't even really see any kind of case here, except Mr. Lill needs to get straight and start getting some help for his drinking problem. I can't see how we can leave the man in here."

She was getting very flustered and she tried to interrupt the judge, but he just continued, "Here's how it's going to go. Mr. Lill, don't do this again, I'm dismissing this case and that's that. Thank you very much."

That prosecutor was so mad because she had it out for me all in the name of domestic violence, even though domestic violence wasn't even close to what happened in that living room. I was mad, sure, but I never abused Amy. I burned a small part of a curtain. Was that stupid? Absolutely. I could've burned the house down, I guess, but becoming violent? I don't think so.

When I got out, I went back to Amy's. We worked things out, and she had a beautiful meal for me and time went on. Eventually, we split up because of yours truly and my alcoholism.

But…I was on my way to turning a corner.

In the back: Ernest Mannis, boat Captain, lived in a tipi for a while. Dead from alcohol. Julie Shanafelt with her catch; no more booze for her, she's doing well.

Julie again, with my favorite girl Mishelle in front. Mishelle died from alcohol. Absolutely heartbreaking for me. Shelly fell down drunk and busted her head on a dresser.

Mishelle and Julie, living it up on a beach in Florida, enjoying the spoils of war. Better days.

Partner John Cole and Mishelle with friend John Pruss - both Johns missing in action! If either of you are out there, contact me! God Bless you both!

My dad Otto, the ass kicker, and my mom, my grandparents, and in the front, l to r, Mike, Greg and me. This is my grandma Lill, who used to feed me the fucking alcohol when I was a kid. I was already having drinks at this age!

Grade school drunk. Me in the 6th grade at Valley Woods Elementary School. I was already drinking heavily!

My brother Mike, the schizophrenic alcoholic, with his new Fender Mustang, my sister Joanne, my mom, and me. Mike dropped dead in a stranger's front yard in Clearwater, Florida. No one with mental issues should be drinking and drugging. God Bless Mike.

l to r: Me, Mike Slesinski, Norm Lyle, Bill Whitney and Blaise Henry, all old pals from my youth. I had just turned 16. Recently Blaise died from the effects of long time alcohol addiction. God Bless Blaise. Bill Whitney has been sober for fifteen years. God Bless Bill.

Me and Kathy Wacker and my mom the day I was released from Oakland County Juvenile Home. They wacked my hair short. After this, I moved to the farm in Southfield.

Here I am in 2019, re-visiting my old stomping grounds at Oakland County Juvenile Home. It has since been closed as a juvenile facility. Not the nicest place to live.

Old friend Jimmy Heidrich. A sad end to an incredibly talented artist. God bless Jimmy.

Me and old friend Bruno Heidrich ("Reefus"), brother of Jimmy, Roy, Gary, a recovering alcoholic, and Glen.

My best friend Brian Schaffer. If not for Brian, I may not be alive today. Dead …alcohol.

Childhood friend Carl Francavilla. He and his brother Bobby are old pals. Both still alive! His mother Fran nursed me back to health after the beating I took in Georgia.

Old friend Roy Heidrich…now sober and taking good care of himself.

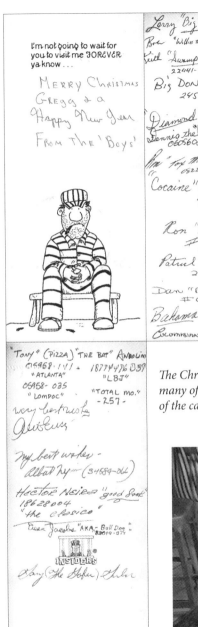

I'm not going to wait for you to visit me FOREVER ya know...

MERRY CHRISTMAS
GREGG & a
Happy New Year
FROM THE 'BOYS'

100 IN-5E   E.R.B. ENTERPRISES©

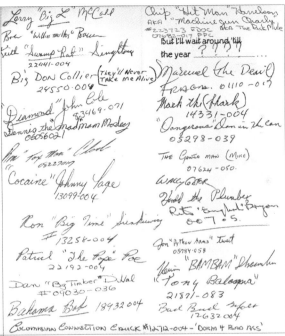

Lenny "Big L" McCall
Bre "Willie mathis" Brown
Keith "Swamp Rat" Singleton
22441-004
Big Don Collier (They'll Never Take me Alive)
24550-004
"Diamond" John Cole
53469-071
Dennis the madman Modes
0606021
Rex "Fox Man" Cloud
0822701
"Cocaine" Johnny Sage
13099-004
Ron "Big Time" Srankuniry
#13258-004
Patrick "The Pope" Poe
22192-004
Dan "Big Timber" DeVal
#09030-036
Bahama Bob 18932004
COLOMBIAN CONNECTION CHUCK #12712-004 - 'DORM 4 BAD ASS'

Chris "Hit Man" Harrison
AKA "Machine Gun Charly" AKA The Pack Mule
#223723 FDOC
07683-017 PPC
But I'll wait around 'till the year ??????...

Marcus (the Devil)
FRAGA. 01110-017
Mach the (Shark)
14331-004
"Dangerous" Dan in the can
05298-039
THE GANJA MAN (MIKE)
07624-050.
WACKY GATOR
Harold the Plumber
R.S. "Everybody's Dragon"
007.5.
Jon "Arthur Arms" Twait
05984-058
Kevin "BAMBAM" Dheenba
"Tony Balogna"
21871-083
Bud Bud Super
12632004

"TONY" (PIZZA) "THE BAT" ANDOLINI
05968-141 - 18774476 D59
"ATLANTA"   "LBJ"
05A58- 035
"LOMPOC"   "TOTAL mo."
       -257-
very best wishes
[signature]

my best wishes -
Albat Ny (34584-066)
HECTOR NSIES "good book"
18628004
"the classics"
Dean Jacobs "AKA - Bull Dog"
83019-071
HUSTLERS®

Gary (The Gofer) Chdr

The Christmas card I sent my brother Greg, signed by many of the inmates, including Aldo Gucci on the back of the card, at Eglin AFB in Ft. Walton Beach.

My brother, Greg Lill. My Hero.

157

Celebrating our success! Unfortunately, the party continued on for too long for all these people...except Julie Shanafelt (second from right) who's doing well—clean, sober and happy.

Ernest, our boat captain.

Mishelle Special, a very cool, very good woman. Toughest woman I ever knew. If women had balls, hers would be the biggest. God Bless you Mishelle. Gone way too soon.

This is the DC6 we used for the West Virginia smuggle, just before we bought it in Nicaragua. We painted over all the Nicaraguan markings. Never thought I'd be looking at it under these circumstances.

Not much to say here but, "Oops!" The burning wreckage after the landing mishap.

West Virginia State Police removing bales of pot from the crash site.

More bales of pot being carried away from the crash site.

Pot plane trial jury to continue deliberations on young Chadwick

By Rosalie Earle

The jury that found four men guilty and two innocent in the pot plane case will continue its deliberations Monday on the fate of Mark Chadwick.

The U.S. District Court jury was still unable to reach a verdict Friday afternoon on the guilt or innocence of the 24-year-old Belle man. The jury has requested and will hear portions of four witnesses' testimony when it reconvenes Monday.

Earlier Friday, James Chadwick, Mark's father, was acquitted of a conspiracy charge. The two defendants, both suspended deputy sheriffs, were accused of being the link in connection in the ill-fated airstrip land an airplane carrying marijuana at Kanawha

Chadwick said he plans where to the Kanawha County Sheriff's Department, where he held the rank of sergeant and was back at work. "I'm going back to be a police officer," he

The jury returned guilty verdicts against four out-of-state men, who were arrested shortly after the marijuana-laden DC-4 crashed June 6, 1979. A fifth man, Russell Kook of Madison, Wis., was acquitted on two charges against him.

Last winter, four other out-of-state men pleaded guilty to their roles in the conspiracy.

U.S. Attorney Robert B. King said the eight convictions ought to be a message to drug entrepreneurs that drug smuggling operations in Southern West Virginia

one count of conspiracy are/Shane Zarintash, 37, of New York City; Marshall Mechanik, 30, of New York City; Steven Riddle, 36, of Louisville, Ky.; and Jerome Lill of Cleveland, Ohio.

Lill, who was charged with being aboard the plane, was also convicted on two counts concerning importing and possessing marijuana. Lill was muddy and injured when he and another man were arrested on Greenbrier Street a few hours after the crash.

The other three men — Zarin

Zarintash — *Convicted*

Lill — *Convicted*

Riddle — *Convicted*

J. Chadwick — *Acquitted*

M. Chadwick — *Undecided*

DiPiero — *Prosecution*

Betts — *Prosecution*

King — *Prosecution*

Some local news articles about the pot plane bust. Jury still out, but finally, they nailed me..

Horsing around with Richard Chosid, my attorney. Thanks Chosid. Lol!

ATTORNEY RICHARD CHOSID, RIGHT, TAKES RIBBING FROM GUILTY CLIENT JERRY LILL
Verdicts Greeted With Little Emotion After Four Days of Deliberations

STEVEN H. RIDDLE
One Of Four Found Guilty

'Pot' Case Sentencing Set Aug. 6

By BILL BYRD
The Daily Mail Staff

The courtroom drama in the "pot case" will resume at least one

Knapp said today.

"These attorneys are tied up so many times in trial work that it's going to be difficult to find one date for all the sentencings. But I promised them I

this of her brother Mark, 35

Because of the lateness of three other attorneys will also be read to the jury. It requested the information to help it reach a verdict.

favorite television programs tomorrow

The judge also issued a stricter gag to others not to discuss the case any way with the jurors.

It won't have to remind you for

Hash smugglers get long terms

NEWARK (AP) — A federal judge yesterday handed out lengthy prison terms to two New Yorkers convicted of conspiring to smuggle $36 million worth of hashish into the country aboard a boat that sank off the coast of Highlands.

U.S. District Judge Herbert J. Stern sentenced Madeline Sarah Wasserman, 31, to 10 years in prison ignoring pleas that a long prison term would deprive her of the right to bear children.

Stern sentenced Shabaz Shane Zarintash, 40, an Iranian citizen, to

15 years in prison and fined him $15,000. Stern ordered that the penalty be served after a five-year sentence for a 1980 marijuana-smuggling conviction in West Virginia.

The two defendants have been held at the federal Metropolitan Correctional Center in New York following their convictions April 21 on two counts of conspiracy, one count of possessing 36,000 pounds of hashish and two counts of attempted possession.

The Feb. 23 indictment followed an 18-month probe launched when

bales of hashish washed ashore in Highlands after the Falcon, an 80-year-old vessel, sank offshore in rough waters in October 1980.

Her ability to have a family is on the line, Ivan Fisher, Wasserman's attorney, noted in asking Stern for leniency.

Stern asked Fisher if his client should be treated differently than a man.

"Yes, because she has not had children," Fisher said. "She would probably never wind up having a child.

"I'm sad about what I've done to my parents, about what I've done to my own life," said the tearful defendant, who was described by an attorney as an "all-American girl."

Assistant U.S. Attorney Robert Fettweis argued that both defendants should be given long prison terms because neither had cooperated with federal authorities after their convictions.

"While I'm extremely sorry for your parents and your family, I re

See Smugglers, page A2

Letting the world know about our prison sentences. They told me they were broke and couldn't help anyone. Yeah…right!

Mishelle Special, Nathan's mother, and my partner, John Cole.

Nathan and his son, Reef.

Norm Lyle with one of the blue bales from the first smuggle of Colombian gold bud.

Brother Greg and I at my store, All My Soaps, Kress Plaza in Sarasota.

Old pal Bill Whitney, carpentry partner, drinking partner, all-around good guy.

l to r: Ernest, our boat captain and John working on our next gig.

"Camelot," our vessel for many Jamaican runs. Made a nice payday possible for me while I was incarcerated. Grubb and Ernest lost the boat when they took it out for a gig without permission. Both landed in jail. Ernest has passed. God Bless Ernest. Grubb? No idea where he is!

My Australian buddy and boat captain, Grubb, and me looking for a safe spot in northern Florida to unload our cargo.

Me, enjoying the fruits of a successful gig.

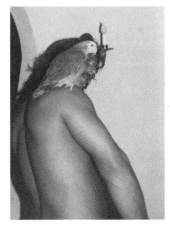

Blitzed on my ass yet again. A genuine fool, not cool!

John fixing the sails and getting ready for another gig.

Julie and John Pruss, and Mike Marsh in the front. Mike is dead too. John? Missing in action. But Julie is alive and well in Florida and completely sober! God Bless all of you!

Me and my German Shepard, Aquarius. in Florida. I was just getting started.

My rottweiler, Charlie Holenhaus. The infamous smuggler dog! The Feds indicted Charlie! Lol!

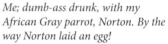

Me; dumb-ass drunk, with my African Gray parrot, Norton. By the way Norton laid an egg!

This is me with my little buddy Blue, who the Lord saw fit to take away from me while I was drunk and not paying attention. Later, Big Fats knocked my ass off a barstool, and put me on a final approach to recovery. Thanks Blue. You saved my life! Haven't had a drink since that day.

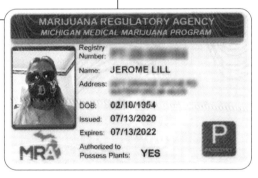

```
Beaumont Health Medical Record
BEAUMONT HEALTH CENTER                          Lill, Jerome O
4949 Coolidge HWY                               MRN: 2308722, DOB: 2/18/1954, Sex: M
Royal Oak MI 48072-1026                         Visit date: 4/22/2016
        04/22/2016 - Office Visit in Beaumont Center for Pain Medicine (continued)

Clinical Notes (continued)
    10-325 MG PO Tab             8 hours as needed for
                                 FOR PAIN or FOR
                                 SEVERE PAIN for up to
                                 30 days. Fill Date:
                                 4/22/2016
                                 Supervising physician
                                 Cain Dimon, MD
                                 DEA#BD8660715
  • morphINE (MS CONTIN) 15 MG PO   take 1 Tab by mouth every   60 Tab   0
    Tab CR                          12 hours for 30 days. Fill
                                    Date: 3-14-16
  • lisinopril (PRINIVIL, ZESTRIL) 20 MG  take 1 Tab by mouth once        0
    PO Tab                         daily.
  • metoprolol (LOPRESSOR) 50 MG PO  take 1 Tab by mouth every            0
    Tab                            8 hours.
  • lorazepam (ATIVAN) 1 MG PO Tab  take 1 Tab by mouth every   21 Tab    0
                                    8 hours.
  • docusate 100 MG PO Cap         take 100 mg by mouth                   0
                                    twice daily as needed for
                                    FOR CONSTIPATION.
  • omeprazole (PRILOSEC) 20 MG PO  take 1 Cap by mouth once              0
    CAPSULE DELAYED RELEASE        daily before dinner.
  • tamsulosin (FLOMAX) 0.4 MG PO Cap  take 1 Cap by mouth once  30 Each  0
                                    every night at bedtime.
  • aspirin 81 MG PO Chew Tab      take 1 Tab by mouth once               0
                                    daily.

No current facility-administered medications for this visit.
```

The list of drugs that were prescribed to me following my leg surgeries. 15 mg of Morphine daily and 90 mg of Vicodin daily—for years.!

My Michigan Medical Marijuana I.D. card. All I can say is, times have sure changed! If we wore these masks back in the day, we'd all be in the slammer Medical marijuana: surely a better choice than alcohol or opiates. Gee, ya think?

During my stay at the Sarasota Salvation Army, following my alcoholic incident and the death of my dog, Blue, I spent part of my days on the back porch, staring at a graveyard directly across the street, knowing deep inside if I continued my reckless behavior, I would soon be part of that real estate.

Dennis Housdorf, left, who died from alcohol, and high rolling fellow scammers at the Columbia Restaurant in Sarasota, Florida. God Bless my good friend Dennis.

Drinking again! IDIOT!

John Cole and one of his workers, "Meathead," looking for a place to unload our cargo for one of our scams that was about to happen.

My fellow bandit Russell on the right, co-conspirator. Very good man, good father and good friend. Sorry we didn't get a chance to patch it up. Russell passed in 2021 from cancer. God Bless Russell and his family

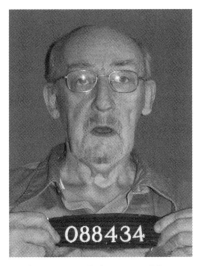

Fucking Harry Shelor. One of the biggest mistakes I ever made was trusting him to do the right thing.

Kentucky State Trooper Daryl Phelps, murdered by Harry Shelor on my pot farm in Kentucky. I still think of him and his family. Still can't forget this tragedy.

Fucking Harry was a bluegrass session musician, believe it or not, and was a founding member of the New Grass Revival, a progressive bluegrass group, and played with Willie Nelson, Waylon Jennings and Leon Russell.

Harry and I went to a bar in Sarasota, The Turtle, and Leon was playing there. Harry and I spent the rest of the evening on Leon's bus. Leon autographed this photo for me.

A break from court at a local Charleston pub. Lawyers, Guns and Money couldn't get me out of this!

OUT FOR POT DEFENSE — The pot plane legal defense team ... defendants gathered at a Capitol Street restaurant for a ... yesterday after the lengthy conspiracy trial went to the jury. ... right are defense lawyers Edwin F. Kagan and Charles Giesen, ... Steven Riddle, Richard Chosid, free-lance illustrator Ann ... Hansbarger, Michael Pollock, ... Kook, Ms. Hansbarger has been ... ative T-shirt marking the yearlong ... Daily Mail Photo by Craig Cunningham

Me buying legal pot in Ann Arbor, Michigan, in early 2020. Is this a great country or what?!

A reminder…always…October 31, 2016…God and Blue decided it was time for me to knock off my drinking and start praying!

Breakfast with my brother Greg, on the left, Greg's friend Jennifer, Bill Sutcliffe and me on the far right in 2018. Stay sober Bill!

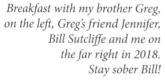

Nathan Special and his son Reef. Nathan, I hope you've learned lessons in your journey from all these loved ones' tragedies. Raise your son well Nathan. Stay straight. Your mom would want you to, and your son depends on it!

The late Jeff Special, Mishelle's brother. Another one gone way too soon. His so-called "friends" just dumped him, dead, in front of the hospital. Heroin!

Mishelle.
Shelley Belly.
Nathan's mom, and
Reef's grandmother.
Truly an angel in my life,
and in the life of any
whose path she crossed.

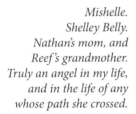

My attorney, Richard Chosid, had this comment printed on buttons during the West Virginia Pot Plane Trial. He quoted Federal Prosecutor Tim Di Piero's statement to Wayne Rich, an assistant prosecutor. We gave a bunch away, and Richard even sold a few. We printed Tshirts also!

491 High Street in Boca Raton, the house I bought with Amy.

The pool on High Street. Too drunk to even notice the angel in the pool when we bought the house!

Me and Amy at the funeral of Jimmy Heidrich, who committed suicide.

The brainchild of Dennis Housdorf and John Cole in St. Pete—Rainbow's End Surf Shop; it died an early death too.

Me, Karen Klucar, Skivvies, and Desiree Smith at the 1981 Kentucky Derby. Desiree was the girl staying with me the night I was raided by the Kentucky State Police when Fucking Harry murdered the State Trooper, Daryl Phelps.

These people, and Karen, below, were definitely angels in my life and still are.

My friend from Kentucky, Karen Smith, and her son and daughter. Her daughter, at the age of 3, was paralyzed from the waist down in an auto accident when her father drove while under the influence—with her in the car—and crashed. She has since successfully forged a career in the entertainment field. Like her mother, a very strong woman who never gave up.

God Bless you all!

In June of 2021, on the 42nd anniversary of the pot plane crash, I returned to Charleston, West Virginia and re-connected with many of the old participants in the crash adventure. Above, l to r: Me, arriving at Yeager Airport (formerly Kanawha County Airport); Stan Bumgardner, Goldenseal Magazine—who made this somewhat odd reunion possible—and me at the airport; Tim DiPiero, former federal prosecutor, and me at the crash site; and finally, my brother Greg and me. I don't need to point out the irony of all this, do I?

CHAPTER ELEVEN

Knocking On Heaven's Door

I went back up to Detroit and continued drinking, but I was doing pretty good. I started working for Adventure MotorHomes, and the owner, Bert Davis, was also a drunk. He had a ton of money and paid me to work for him so I did that, continued on drinking too much, fought with my girlfriend, Amy — my typical self.

I soon started a little remodeling company and worked for a lot of people in the suburbs of Detroit. Actually, right in the area where I used to live. All those neighbors started hiring me, so I had instant work. I did that. I drank, but not obsessively. Still an alkie, though, don't get me wrong. Just waiting for my next shot.

I went out with my friend Roy Heidrich, Jimmy's older brother, who was also an alcoholic. See, I knew a lot of alcoholics. That's who we hung around with, you understand?

So Roy lived above a bar in Hamtramck called The Attic. He lived with a girl named Pam, a fellow alcoholic of his and they would go downstairs and play music. Roy's a musician and a real good guy.

Well, I was working, making pretty good money and living in Royal Oak, and I met this guy named Patrick. He was, like, an interior decorator, designer, full painting, all kinds of shit. We decided to go down to Hamtramck and see Roy play. And sometimes when I drink, I get with Roy and play harmonica, and we jam a little bit.

Well, I got down to The Attic — and this is in, like, '98, I think — and he's on stage fiddling with his slide guitar. And so we just started to jam. I sat at the end of the bar when I first came in, and there's this guy next to me. I had a cell phone — you know, cell phones were fairly new then, and he asked me if he could use my phone. I said yeah, sure, but don't let anybody take my phone and don't let anybody use it. Boy, I didn't know how this was going to turn out. I was drunk.

I go up onstage with Roy and we're playing the Doors' "Roadhouse Blues", and all of a sudden, bam! Gunshots! Everybody in the bar knows what gunshots are. Everybody lays down, hits the deck. And we jump off the stage and see what's going on.

And I go back towards where the guy is with my phone, and there's the guy laying there…dead.

He's deader than a doornail, and my phone — his hand is out, half cupped, and the phone is laying right outside his hand. Now Patrick says to me, "Are you going to get your phone?"

I said, "Shit no, I'm not going to get my phone, you dummy. Let's get the fuck out of here."

So just as we got out, naturally, the cops showed up all over the place and closed the joint down. Apparently the guy got killed because he wouldn't let another guy use my telephone. That was why they were arguing. The newspapers said they had an argument, but I'm telling you what they argued about. I never saw the guy that shot him. I only saw him from the back. A couple other guys were in there, too, but I didn't know them. I told him not to go loaning my phone out, and he died for my phone.

See, whenever you're out getting drunk and doing stupid shit, a lot of things can happen to you that you have no idea are out there for you. So alcoholics can just get in trouble, and it'll find your ass, believe me. If you don't think so, wait and see, because I want you to *stop this shit now.* That's why I'm telling these different stories. I mean, there's nothing but trouble that comes along with substance abuse, period.

I went to a strip club down on Eight Mile Road one afternoon to get drunk for the day. I had been making money doing carpentry. Anyway, it was about 4:00 in the afternoon, and I went to the bathroom.

There's a little bar outside the bathroom, like a service bar. I was sitting there — standing there, actually — drinking, and my wallet was lying on the bar, along with a cocktail. I was still tooting coke back then. So there I was sniffing coke, drinking, and looking to pick up a stripper, which was one of my bad habits that went with my alcoholism.

One of many.

I went to the bathroom, and there's this big, thick guy. He almost looked like Mr. T. Big, gold chains around his neck. And, you know, I stood up to the urinal next to him. We both said, "Hey" to each other, you know, acknowledged each other.

Well, I came walking out of the bathroom, and these two guys came walking towards the bathroom, and they had, like, long duster coats on. I mean, at a fast pace of speed they walked right past me. And I went back out to my little spot at the service bar, right outside the bathroom door.

Bam, bam! Gunshots again, okay?

See, I walk into this shit when I do stupid shit. That's what happens. And it can happen to you, too. It might not happen at a strip club, but you go out there drinking and carousing and not being a good person, and you'll come across something, believe me. It'll happen to you. Believe me, God's watching your ass, trust me. Anyhow, the two guys come out, and they step up because the runway went right down the center of the bar, where the girls danced, you know.

They stopped right in front of me, looked at me, and one of them pointed the gun right at me. I was leaning down because I heard the gunshots, and I'm thinking, *oh, shit*. I thought he was going to shoot me. And then he just lifted it back up, and they continued down the runway and out the door.

My heart was in my mouth.

Stumbling out of the bathroom comes the huge guy that was in there. He's holding the back of his neck, bleeding all over the place. I had a black leather jacket on and a white shirt and black leather pants. He's leaning against the bar, and he's asking to use my phone.

I'm putting napkins on the back of his head — blood pouring out of the lower part of his neck, actually — to stop him from bleeding, keeping pressure on it and someone from the club called an ambulance.

Anyway, this guy wants to use my phone.

Here's my phone. I give him my phone.

He gets on the phone, and he starts calling some friends of his and telling them, in gang language, nicknames and stuff, who it was. So he's calling somebody on my phone to get revenge, and he's bleeding like a pig. I'm trying to sop up the blood until EMS arrives to take over. The cops come and they want to get him on a gurney. This guy is fighting with the cops. He doesn't want to go. He wants to go get the shooters. He was some kind of gang dealer or something, because he was dressed nice and he had a ton of good gold on him. I know the look.

So anyhow, they made us stay there all night long, until like, 2:00 in the morning, questioning if anybody saw anything. And the strippers had told the cops that I was in the bathroom just before this guy got shot.

Great.

I asked them if I could go home, and they said I wasn't going anywhere until I started remembering. Well, my memory was not good, and they finally let me go. I mean, here's moment when my guardian angels – you've got guardian angels too – were watching over me. You can bet your ass on that. Eventually, though, they're going to let their guard down and you're going to get kerplunked. I can tell you that right now.

A prosecutor in my trial, Tim DiPiero, during his closing argument, said to the jury, "When you live right, things go right. When you're not living right, things go wrong." I never forgot that message. He left a definite impression on me.

My Grandma Klump, almost 100 years old, told me that kind of stuff. Slowly, I'm beginning to understand that, sometimes, living right and living wrong take a conscious effort. Life doesn't just happen to you. Sometimes, life is about the choices you make.

Mr. Frayden was a guy I worked for in Sarasota, Florida back in my 30s or 40s. He owned Six Flags and was an attorney. I did some work on his house, and I told him I was going to write a book. He told me, "You can't write a book yet. You don't know enough."

And I didn't. Yet.

Mr. Frayden got involved with Six Flags by turning left when he should have turned right. He had just got out of college. If you're living right, things'll go right for you. When you're living wrong, it's not that anybody's after you, except for God, and he's only trying to teach you. So, you know, shit, man, see the signs. Don't put yourself through the crap I went through.

I'm trying to help you out. You know, you can't have a drink if you're trying to quit drinking. Just start praying to God. He'll help you out. You don't need to take that drink. Once you take that drink, you're fucked. Excuse my language again. I'm trying not to use that word as much, but sometimes it just flies out, because it's the only thing that explains how I feel.

Mishelle Special had called to tell me that Dennis had died. His brother was trying to get a hold of him, and he wasn't answering his phone. So his brother went and checked on him, and no one would answer the door. He had a key so he let himself in. He found Dennis immediately in a chair. He had bled out.

Now, bleeding out is not a pretty sight. That is what alcohol can do to you. Your liver, your insides, will burst and pop, and you will bleed out of your ass, your nose, all of your orifices will bleed. You don't want to die that way, and you don't want anybody to find you that way.

My good friend, Dennis Housdorf, at 52 years old, was gone.

I kept meeting with Mishelle, calling her, and attempting to help her cut back on drinking. But she was living with another alcoholic, and, you know, alcoholics like to hang out together because they've got to have somebody to drink with. Or you'll drink alone.

Anyway, Mishelle kept it up. I couldn't really help Mishelle because I'm still a drunk. That doesn't really work. So this should help you a little bit if you want it to.

Go exercise. Do good things. Go help people. Quit feeling sorry for yourself. That's a bunch of bullshit.

One night, Mishelle got so drunk — she drank, like, one of those liters of vodka, or something near that — and she fell over and banged her head on her dresser drawers.

They found her dead.

So that was the end of my dear friend, Mishelle. Alcohol. I mean, the list goes on, of all these people that just die, constantly, from this shit. It'll kill you, too. That's why I call this the book A Battle of Angels; because you've got good sides and bad sides. You should listen to the song "Battle Of Angels" by John Mellencamp. It's a song that I can reflect on my life with, remember all of my friends who died too young, and consider how blessed I am to have this chance to live a new life and spread love.

So dig this, man. You want to know how I got sober? October of 2016, I had been back up in Michigan, and I'd been living with a woman, a good friend of mine. Her name was Sue. Sue was really good to me, and I had some bad operations on my legs, because after my airplane crash, my legs had always bothered me. I had damaged the arteries in my legs so I had femoral popliteal bypass surgeries. Plus, my heavy drinking and smoking — my lifestyle — wasn't making things any easier.

I had two nine-hour operations on each leg, which took a lot of rehab. Physically, I was bouncing back pretty good, except I was still drinking. This time, though, I got to have pain pills. Vicodin and morphine. I had Ativan, too, which is used so you don't shake, but I was using it just as a tranquilizer for anxiety. I also was smoking pot.

In hindsight, I should have just been smoking pot, but I was using everything. Pot wasn't what was making me nuts, it was the other drugs, the combination, that was making me nuts. Needless to say, I wasn't very nice to Sue, and I wasn't very happy with my life so I knew I needed a change.

I had a little blue Pomeranian — a little teacup — Blue, my best buddy for about 7 or 8 years. He was a good little dog. I went down to Sarasota, Florida, to care for the mother of a friend of mine and rent a room at her house. It was just down the street from my brother Gregory's, nursing home, too, so it was going to be nice seeing him more often. I knew I should be there more often, so I decided to just move there, get out of Detroit, change my lifestyle, and, you know, start over.

Annie Moss, my friend's mother, was in a nursing home getting rehabbed after breaking her hip. She was going to need assistance when she came back home so I went down there to do that since I was recovering as well.

While she was in the nursing home, instead of occupying myself with important things, I had the whole house, and I just decided to get drunk. And that's exactly what I did. I'd just go to the nursing home now and then, but I basically concentrated on watching TV and eating Vicodin, morphine, and Ativan.

And getting drunk on vodka.

Anyway, on Halloween of 2016, I got up and naturally, I had my cocktails. And I'm dicking around, and Annie had come home from the nursing home, and she's got a little bit of craziness in her. She was banging on my door wanting me to take her somewhere or do something, I don't really know.

Blue was up on my bed. I was drunk and not paying attention or maybe just completely out of it. My dog got nasty barking because he was trying to protect me. He dove off the bed, and smashed head first into a doorwall to the side of my bed. He broke his neck and died right in front of me. Yeah. Think how that makes you feel.

If I had been paying attention, my dog probably wouldn't have died. My dog committed suicide, as far as I'm concerned, because he was sick and tired of living with my ass. I tried to give him mouth-to-mouth. No dice. He was dead. So I sat there.

Now my dog's dead. I'm drunk, eating Vicodin and morphine, and, you know, I decided I was going to drink myself to death. But here's the deal on that. I've been drinking myself to death since I was a kid, since my dad kicked the shit out of me. I was running around doing drugs in Detroit and the suburbs, going to concerts. The whole time I was drinking like that, I'd been trying to kill myself.

When we're drinking like this, we're suicidal. When you're taking all these drugs and you do substance abuse, you're just numbing yourself because you're not happy. You've got inner problems. You're not going to fix them by doing this shit, okay? Feeling sorry for yourself or wanting to kill yourself, you're not fixing anything. You might become numb but you're not helping yourself in the least — not at all. You're making things worse and it's going to come to a head.

That was the moment I decided I was going to drink myself to death. I disposed of my dog and I decided I was just going to finish myself off that day.

That's it. I'm done. I thought I couldn't take it anymore, the sadness, the pain. I couldn't numb myself enough to forget it all. I called a friend of mine who owned a cab company in Sarasota, had him take me to a bar over by the airport called Memories where I used to drink.

Well, I went in there—I had a pocket full of $100 bills—and I was just going to drink and buy other people drinks. I was going to actually commit suicide with alcohol poisoning. I knew I could drink myself to death, I'd been trying for years, but now I figured this time I'm really going to pull it off. I decided I had nothing left to live for—my little buddy was dead, my friends were dying, and I've lost a lot over my years.

I just flat out gave up and I was going to die.

I eventually tired of drinking at Memories, so I called another cab and had him drive me to some bar over by Lockwood Ridge. I started buying everybody drinks, ordering double rum and ginger ales, vodka this, tequila that, and shots of anything the bartender would make.

I bought all kinds of drinks. The next thing I know I'm in the hospital on a stretcher, completely out of it. I do remember the EMS guys around me, and they told me that I had croaked. I guess my heart was skipping. I had gotten a concussion and they gave me CAT scans. I don't remember that part but I do know that's what happened. Because my blood alcohol was so high, they couldn't let me back in public.

In Florida, they've got a thing called the Marchman Act, which means you have to go straight to a rehab facility if you come to the hospital as an alcoholic. So they took me to a place called First Step. It's a rehab/detox center, but they've got to dry you out first. It's a detox center, and they won't let you out until you meet expectations.

Detoxing is a nasty experience and process. I was in and out of consciousness, and when I finally came to, I looked in the mirror and I had a black eye from smacking my head so hard. The DTs were coming now and your skin is going to feel like it's turning inside out. Anybody who's gone through withdrawals from alcohol knows how serious this is. It's not something you should play with if you're going to quit drinking and you're really addicted. You should do it medically because chances are you'll break down and go get a drink. Then you just start all over and you say I'll do it again tomorrow, I'll just start tomorrow.

You never start. Tomorrow never comes. There's always another drink and then you're screwed.

Anyhow, I met protocol at the detox facility, I think, after eight or nine days. That's how long it took for them – for me – to get right. They were tranquilizing me so I wasn't shaking or having tremors too bad, because I've had seizures from that. They got me sobered up and then it was time for me to leave.

I asked for my wallet, which I knew had a bunch of hundreds in it, but guess what? My wallet was empty. I was sure there had been at least one more $100 bill tucked in there.

They told me which way I could go to get to 301 to head home, or I could go over to the Salvation Army and see if I could get into a rehabilitation program. When I came out of there, I was either going to go left or right.

This is where I remember Mr. Frayden telling me decisions are either left or right in your life. He also told me I had to live more — see more — before I could write a book. Well, he was right, and now I'd seen enough.

I was thinking about going to California and seeing some friends, or going back up to Detroit. I had some money in the bank, I wasn't broke, but I didn't really want to drink any more because I just had this shit kicked out of me enough.

I mean, come on. God knocked me off the bar stool, that's a fact.

This is the moment I heard His message, loud and clear. So I turned toward the Salvation Army and I met this guy named DeShawn who ran the program.

I told him that I was dried out, but that I wanted to stay sober. I knew if I went back out on the streets and rented some place, I would go straight back to the bottle. I needed help and DeShawn was there to help me. It had cost me too much already, and I almost paid the largest price you can pay and that was with my life. I could've left my brother alone in the nursing home.

What a fucking asshole I was. I mean, that's basically all I can say.

I started working this 30-day quality of life program and, basically, you just have to hang out and be straight and sober and try to get out in society and get a job. I wasn't looking for a job because I received disability, my legs are shot, and really there's not much I can do in the carpentry business. But I was determined to pull myself together. It's the whole reason I went into this program at the Salvation Army, and I stayed there.

I did the 30-day deal and, as I was in there, I met a couple of other people that were alkies to my extent. They had bad problems, but they hadn't done as much as I had — I mean I was a toasted alcoholic.

I was a professional, let's put it that way.

Anyway, I met this guy named Dave in the program; he's a veteran from the Gulf War, and he's got a drug problem and a cocaine problem. He's there trying to get himself right, the veterans are helping him find a place to live. I didn't want to leave there just yet because I knew I wasn't ready. I was going to really fix myself this time — fix myself for good, and I did.

When I was in the hospital with alcohol poisoning, I had lost my cross that I wore every day. I wanted to find it, it was a comfort to me. I called Sarasota Memorial Hospital and told them my name, what and when everything happened. They transferred me to Lost and Found, and the woman on the phone told me to wait a minute while she checked the vault.

She said "Well, Mr. Lill, if you come down here I've got your cross and I've got your money. You can come on over and pick it up." I got in a taxi cab and I went right down to the Sarasota Memorial Hospital, and she came out with a Zip-Lock bag with all my $100 bills in it and my cross.

Now…you tell me I have no guardian angels? Bullshit.

If I'm not convinced that God's watching my ass by now, then I'm a complete idiot. I mean, let's really look at the situation, these are not coincidences. The woman who worked at lost and found helped me put the necklace on and, as she did, she said, "Somebody is watching out for you, you must have something to do."

That didn't really register with me right then. As I filed that message away in the back of my brain, I walked outside. I saw a guy in a red jacket, dirty as can be, his hands were shaking, all beat up. I asked him what happened and he told me somebody jumped him and beat him up. He was an old drunkard—actually, he probably wasn't that old, maybe 40, 45—but he looked rough as hell and he was shaking. A lifetime of alcohol and drug problems will age a man far quicker than a normal lifestyle will.

He wanted to know if I had a couple of bucks and, for a minute, I was going to give him some money. I mean, I had that money I just picked up from Lost and Found, plus a few other bucks in my pocket. Something told me that he was just going to walk right across the street to the store and get some liquor. I just knew it. If I gave this guy some money, I'm just helping him continue on a terrible path.

Turning and walking away, I said to myself, *no, I'm not going to give it to him.* A split second later, I turned around for a glimpse of the guy, and he's gone. I have no idea where he went so fast.

You know what I think that was? That was Evil, right there, seeing what I was going to do — testing me. You hear about God and the Devil, light and dark, a higher power — whatever it is you call it — every day right now.

I'll tell you one thing: God's on one side, and all you've got to do to be on that side is be good. That's it. That's the only rule involved as far as I'm concerned. You can't be on His side when you're drinking. You may say, "Oh, I'm a good person and I do this," but you're not being a good person when you're drunk or on drugs. You're being an abusive person. Being abusive doesn't mean you only abuse others. Sure, as an abuser you bring others down, but the person you hurt the most is yourself. I made the choice to stop abusing myself.

I had decided I was going to be sober and I was ready to fight for it. Dave eventually found a house because the Veterans were going to give him some money to get into this place. He had the first and last month's payments ready to go, and asked if I could come up with some money so we could get this house together. The woman who rented it seemed very nice, and now I'm sober and I'm feeling pretty good about my future. I hadn't been sober that long now, only three months or so, but I wasn't having any urges for alcohol, believe me.

I wasn't there but a couple of weeks when I came back to the house after visiting my brother and working out at the YMCA. I started exercising a lot, which I'd done quite a bit in my life. Exercise is a great substitute for alcohol or drugs. Exercise is important in your recovery, and I preoccupied myself with that and seeing my brother more often.

Anyway, when I came home Dave told me that this woman is being foreclosed on. This is tourism season in Sarasota, Florida, which means you can't find shit to rent at that time of the year. Everything is expensive and you just — it's ridiculous. So I was, like, oh no, now I've got to go find a place. I was doing my laundry outside and I was praying by the laundry machines at this little guest house.

The next morning I planned to start looking for places to stay. I'm telling God, you know, come on Big Fats—that's another nickname I had for God—you've got to help me, man. I'm not going to drink any more, I promised you that, because it cost my dog his life, I wasn't seeing my brother right, I've been living wrong all these years, come on and help me out. I could use a sign that He heard me.

When I finished my laundry, I walked down the driveway to go start searching for a place. Two houses down was an older guy, big black truck parked out front and a couple fancy cars parked in the street. I noticed that he was moving things from his house to another one two doors down. I've seen him before and we had been friendly in the past. I said hello to him and just let him know that my landlady was foreclosed on.

We had some small talk and I moved on to look for a place. At first I wasn't happy about my landlady not telling us she was foreclosed on and giving us very little time to make arrangements for a new place to stay. I guess she was in trouble so I just started praying for her. I'm not mad at her; I don't get mad at people anymore, that's another thing.

Get rid of your anger, that will help you.

So, I'm pretty bummed because I couldn't find anything; it's all too expensive. I mean, I only get, like, $800 a month Social Security and that doesn't buy you much. Defeated, I came back home.

The next day, I tried again. The older guy was outside again, unloading his stuff, and he called me over. He told me to follow him to the backyard. He showed me a little tiny guest house behind this house. He said, "I don't know what you pay there, but you could probably rent this."

I said, "I don't know if I could afford that." Remember, this is Sarasota, Florida. It's high dollar, especially during the tourist season. I didn't think in any way that I could afford it, but he said, "Well, you could rent this and pay what you're paying there." I was paying $400 or $500, so I jumped at the offer and said, "Fine, I'll do that." I only had to go a couple houses over after praying my ass off, and I moved right in.

He was kind of a wacky guy and I ended up helping him with his dog when he needed me to take care of him. I didn't mind, though, because I love dogs. Eventually, I moved on from there, but it was a great break for me at the time. This was not a stroke of luck, believe me. Everything started working out for me as soon as I sobered up and quit drinking. God knocked me off that bar stool and that was the last time He was going to put up with my shit.

Earlier, I mentioned a man named Walt who owned Walt's Fish Market. He helped me when I had no money and made sure I had food. Well, at the end of my street was another Walt's Fish Market and that's where I met his grandson, Brett. He's a helluva guy. I walked by there on my way in and out from running errands, and we became friends. He invited my brother and me to his birthday party, which excited the hell out of my brother. I see this as another case of positive energy in this world, because his grandfather was good to me, and now I meet this guy and he's good to me. Clearly, this is a very good family and I was meant to know both of these men.

I got my health back and I dried my ass up. Mishelle's son Nathan had a bout with alcoholism and he's now sober as well. He had messed up pretty bad, which scared him back on the wagon. It's not uncommon for children of alcoholics to start drinking at a very early age. His mom was a big-time alcohol and drug abuser and she dropped dead. He didn't have a great role model, didn't really have a male role model at all, and I tried to help him best I could.

We all have a chance to make the right decision. I mean you're getting opportunities to make a choice every single day. It might even be why you bought this book. Sometimes the choice you need to make is a no-brainer — it's obvious. Other times, it's tough to weigh out the options. The best thing you can do in that scenario is pray. Anytime you want to have a drink, pray. If you're feeling particularly down on yourself, pray.

Pray for yourself, pray for others. Just pray.

I don't care if you feel stupid or you think that's nuts, because it will work. If you believe in that, you're going to be cured. Take advice from me and don't do that shit.

Alcoholism is an ugly way to die, too. I don't think you really want to die that way. You can say, "Oh, that's not going to happen to me."

Bullshit.

There are a lot of positive, productive things you can find to do that don't involve drinking. Visit or volunteer at a nursing home. Play sports. Start a garden or pick up a hobby. Just don't pick up a drink. Let my words echo in your head. If nothing else, pray your ass off, because you'll get an answer. By the time you're finished praying, that feeling for that drug or that alcohol will pass. I know it's hard, but I'm telling you, if I can quit drinking, so can you.

CHAPTER TWELVE

Journey To the Center of the Mind

My journey to sobriety had a significant turning point when I began seeing my brother, Gregory, every day. Gregory is very special and, like I said, a major drive for me to remain sober and keep my shit together. Every day I marched down the street, caught the bus, picked up Gregory, and we went to the YMCA. We exercised together every day, which is another important factor in my sobriety these past years.

Gregory is 71 years old, has cerebral palsy, epilepsy, mildly mentally disabled, and bound to a wheelchair. He's also probably one of the finest human beings and most influential people that I've ever known because, when you go to these nursing homes, you see these people who are sitting around with nothing to do. They've got a lot of health problems, some have lost limbs, some have been in bad accidents, some have had strokes, you name it. I mean, they are dealing with a billion things, but I challenge any substance abuser to walk into a nursing home and look at those people in the eye and tell me you don't feel sorry for taking your life for granted. These people don't have the luxury of just getting up and going wherever they like. They can't walk into a grocery store to pick up some necessities. People who live in nursing facilities would love to be you, would love to have your freedoms. Yet, people who turn to drugs or alcohol just feel sorry for themselves and all the problems that come along with substance abuse. Little do you know, you could be exactly the person your friend or family member needs. Gregory needed me to be healthy for him. I made the decision to be there for him by putting aside my selfishness.

My brother and I found an activity to do together which helped refocus my mind and body: we exercised. I built strength of mind and body through exercising with my brother. He's one of the strongest human beings I know and he was a big motivator for me to keep going. He was born into a life of health problems and he's maintained the most positive attitude through all of his 71 years. He's still going strong. I asked him what keeps him going and keeps his mindset positive and he said it was all thanks to prayer and trusting in God.

Looking back at my previous visits, I remember seeing him and my mother praying every night. I wish I had dropped to my knees with them because maybe I would've heard God talking in that silence. Maybe I wasn't ready to let go of the noise in my head and listen to the stillness of my heart just yet.

I'm not claiming my whole life was full of bad times, I had some good and enjoyable moments, too. Those good times probably would've been better had I not been drunk off my ass, but I'll never truly know.

Discovering a life of sobriety took at least a year before my brain really cleared out — no booze, no drugs, no Ativan, not even pot — I completely cleaned my head out. It takes a whole year before your brain even starts to think right, I can tell you that much. So you've got to give it a chance. You're not ready to really claim sobriety just because you've been dry for four months or six months. I mean, you still have things going wrong with your brain, believe me.

It's difficult to get sober alone. You need a support network that fits with you and, sometimes, medical help is important, because you want to live, you don't want to die trying.

I'm a year into sobriety and a situation fell into my lap on Christmas Eve in 2017. I was planning to go see Gregory during the day and I always call him before I leave to make sure he's available.

He wasn't answering any of my calls so I was thinking he's either out or on the toilet. Gregory has got some problems with his intestines, so he's on the toilet a lot of the time. I called again and nothing. He's still not answering his phone, so decided to go to the dollar store and buy some super glue to fix a wooden cross that had broken.

I made the short trek down the street to the bus stop and hopped on the next bus. I got my glue, picked up a couple things from the grocery store, and went back to the bus stop to head home. I was sitting down at the bus stop and traffic's super heavy, and I heard this clinkity clink, thump, thump, thump. I turned to my left and saw this Jeep Wagoneer limping up, with a flat tire. It already had a donut tire on it, and a little, short girl sitting behind the wheel. Her head was down, so I got up to see if she was okay. As I walked over, she got out of the car and just stood there, staring at her car. I said, "Doesn't look good. You got a spare tire?" Of course she didn't because it was already on the car. She'd been driving on the spare for a while, and I asked her where she was headed.

I could smell alcohol on her, no doubt about that.

I had assumed that she probably lived in Sarasota, so we somehow could get her home at least. She started in on a sad story about how she had just dropped some guy off that threatened her and scared her; it was Christmas Eve and she was supposed to get presents for her kids. She started crying. She almost made me cry with her story. I let her put her head on my shoulder and I thought, I've got to do something here. What that was, I wasn't sure, but I was going to do something. I told her, "Everything's going to be okay," but I don't actually know whether I thought it was or not.

I asked, "Have you ever ridden on a bus?

She said, "No, I don't even know how to ride on a bus."

"Well, if you ride with me, I'll take you just a little ways up here."

She had a lot of balls to go with me. I could've been anything — a killer, a rapist, anything. She's lucky she ran into me that day, that's for sure. We took the bus up a little ways so we could go to a tire center, but they couldn't do anything for her because they didn't have what she needed in stock. I figured the best thing to do at this point was to just get her home because she was drunk; I could smell alcohol all over the girl. She didn't need to be driving even if we could get her car repaired.

I asked, "Well, where do you live?" assuming it was somewhere in Sarasota.

She said, "I live on Anna Maria Island." That's about 35 miles away.

I asked her what she was doing out this way, and she told me the story about this guy named Drew, who she had met in rehab. Now I'm getting the story about her, because I know she's drunk. I can smell it all over her, and she shouldn't be driving a car.

"Listen," I said, "I'll get you some money and you can use my AAA Gold Card to get your car home." I had just got AAA so I could have other people's cars towed in an emergency when I was with them, because I'm an old geezer now and my legs aren't in great shape. We grabbed the bus back to her car, which was also at the end of my street, and I walked to my house — only five houses away from the bus stop.

I grabbed a couple hundred bucks and my new AAA card. When I walked back she wasn't where I left her and I panicked a little because she was pretty drunk. Drunk enough to get in some trouble, I'll tell you. I tried to explain what I wanted to do and she kept interrupting me.

I said, "Now, listen, listen, shut the fuck up." I mean, I hate to say it, but she wouldn't listen, and I told you that 'fuck' gets the point across. I don't even know this girl, right, she just looked at me like, *what is with this guy?*

I said, "You've got to listen to me. I'm going to call AAA, I'm going to get a car carrier, and I'm going to get your vehicle taken all the way back to your house."

I called AAA and made the arrangements. After a while, the tow truck showed up, and the driver said, "You're lucky because I wasn't going to take the call. I figured that I could do one more since it was Christmas Eve." God was watching out for this lady.

She wanted to give me her driver's license as a sign of good faith, and I said, "Look, if you're going to keep my AAA card and keep my $200, no big loss to me. I've lost a lot more than that in my life, believe me, honey." She had no idea who I was or what I'd done, so I didn't need her driver's license or anything, I just wanted to get her home.

The driver loaded the Jeep onto the tow and I watched them drive away.

I had given her my phone number so she could return my money and AAA card, even though I wasn't expecting to get either of them back. I felt pretty good about what I had done, even though most of the people I told didn't think it was going to work out for me.

The next morning — Christmas Day — and my phone rings. This lady had called me up and thanked me over and over, and told me she was going to pay me back as soon as the banks were open the next day. I told her I was just glad she made it home because she was in no state to be driving or roaming around. She insisted she wasn't drunk, and I said, "From one alcoholic to another, I know you were."

She responded with, "Well, I wasn't that drunk."

Yeah, she was that drunk.

I hopped on the bus to head out toward her house on Anna Maria Island. I found her house easily enough and she let me in. I walked in and saw she had my AAA card and money ready to go on the table. We made small talk and she thanked me some more. I mentioned something about drinking and she made it out to be that this was a one-time thing, she didn't normally do that. I could feel the energy of alcoholism 100%, though. I mean, her kids are gone, for one. They left to be with their father on Christmas Eve. That doesn't typically happen if it's a one-time thing.

I came right out and asked, "So, how long have you been drinking on this little binge?"

She was a little caught off guard, but admittedly said, "Well, I just had gotten out of rehab and then I started drinking again."

There it is: rehab.

I knew she was in trouble because she's a true alcoholic. She tried to insist she wasn't and that she was just sad about her divorce, blah, blah, blah. I knew she was trying to talk her way out of me thinking she's an alcoholic. I just wanted to help this girl a lot. Act of God, divine intervention, call it what you want, but it's real. She needed to dry out and no one should do it alone.

I said, "You're going to probably be shaking."

She looked a little nervous and said, "Well, I know, I've had that before. I don't want to go through that."

"Well you're going to have to go through it. If you want me to come around and hang around a little bit, just to get you through the process."

I wasn't trying to pick this girl up, believe me. I just really wanted to help her because she needed it. She was a beautiful girl and I love beautiful women, but I had no eyes set on this girl for that intention. I stayed with her through her shakes, and she dried out. When your body goes through withdrawals, you can't eat, you'll throw up what little bit you do eat, you lose control of yourself. It's a difficult thing to experience.

We became friends once she was dried out and she could have conversations. One thing led to another and we kind of became more than friends, let me put it that way. I had no aspirations to do this whatsoever, but shit happens, as we say. Anyway, she became my best friend for a year, and I continuously stayed with her and we started to do pretty well.

Her mother had lived next door, and I began to understand why this girl was an alcoholic. It's a common story so many of us share. Mother is an alcoholic, parents fought often, father had an affair, and the child witnesses everything.

Her mother hired a private investigator to get pictures of her father with the other woman and then she showed the pictures to my friend when she was a little girl. As I listened to her recall memories, I couldn't help but think about my own past as a young man who was often beaten by his father. I didn't see my dad with other women, but anything we see when we're young, affects us. And you've got to remember, her dad was a drinker, her grandfather was a drinker, her mother was a drinker, it's in the genes.

I figured the best thing I could do for myself is to stay occupied by helping somebody else with the same problem. I'm still very glad I did this for this young lady. Her mother wasn't so fond of me helping her daughter out, but let's be real; she doesn't have a right to say that to me because she played a big role in her daughter becoming an alcoholic. She became a great friend of mine over the year I spent helping her stay sober. She had several setbacks and eventually went into rehab.

I had to learn a lot about this family as the year went on. One of the things I learned was that this girl had a multifaceted addiction. I saw signs of a lot of mental illness, which by no means is anything to be embarrassed about, or to think you're "less than" because of it. So many people have mental health issues and, unfortunately, there is a negative stigma. One day I hope that changes so people are willing to ask for the help they need. For alcoholics and substance abusers, we find ways to self medicate, to numb our feelings.

I've dealt with depression for most of my life and drinking was my way out of that hole, but instead of opening myself up, I was burying myself into a deeper hole of depression. It's a lonely, heavy feeling. The weight is too much to bear sometimes but there are people who want to help you.

Anytime you can help a fellow addict or substance abuser, don't hesitate to jump in there because they're alone and, at one point or another, we all experience loneliness. Help and inspire them to make positive choices, celebrate the little things, look at sobriety one day at a time, one hour at a time if you really need to.

You've just got to trust yourself and trust in God.

Pray, pray, pray your ass off. It will get you through every moment that you want to take a drug or drink. If you start praying you'll forget about that drink in a few short minutes actually. It doesn't take long.

Of course, I continued to visit my brother in the nursing home, and I enjoyed entertaining all the residents. I had made friends with the bingo club and I brought food to share. They enjoyed my company as much as I enjoyed theirs. You know, I was inspired by a movie that I always liked, "The Untouchables." Kevin Costner, as Eliot Ness, said to his partner that he's going to break up the crime family, Al Capone and all that shit, and he says to the other guy, "Now let's go do some good."

That's what I started telling myself every morning: let's go do some good.

So I marched on every day and I would say, "Let's go do some good." I also prayed while I walked everywhere, which I started walking most days. Well, actually I limped around most days because my two bad legs made me look like a Limp-Along Cassidy.

I realize that I can't save the world, but maybe a couple of people will listen to this shit and go out and do some good. Don't do so much that you overburden yourself. You could easily slip back if you feel too overwhelmed, so take it slow — one day, one hour, one minute at a time. Whatever it takes.

Don't take it lightly. You've got a big job to do if you're going to quit this crap and if you know somebody that's doing it, stick with them and help them. I've got a lot of friends who I thought had ditched me, but it was actually me who pushed them away. They couldn't do anything for me because I wasn't allowing them to. That's the key: you must be willing to submit to God's plans. If you're battling alcoholism, allow people to be a support for you and pray every day.

God responds to all of his angels, you just have to listen.

Sad Clowns and Hillbillies

I came to Detroit, Michigan, on April 2, 2019, with the plan to share these episodes from my life about drug and alcohol abuse, along with some of my smuggling experiences to entertain a little bit. I also wanted to show what the not-so-glamorous side of abuse and smuggling is all about. In short, it's not a good lifestyle to lead and there will be a lot of loss, a lot of friends will die.

After I finished recording the beginning of this book, I took off to go see a friend of mine who I was in trouble with in Charleston, West Virginia. He's an ex-cop. His name is Mark Chadwick, and he was charged in my case. I stopped by to see him and his wife, Karen, in East Lansing. He gave me a few pictures that he had from the crash, which we both experienced. He was accused of being paid off in my case. For the record, I never paid him anything.

Then I decided to go up north and see my old friend Roy Heidrich again. I mentioned his brother, Jimmy Heidrich, who had committed suicide. Well, Roy had been an alcoholic ever since. He lives up in

Hillman, Michigan, and he's a really good guy. So I went up to see Roy to try to help him out because I could tell when I called him he was pretty smashed.

When I arrived, I discovered a pretty bad disaster area, and we got it cleaned up. It took me almost the whole summer. But I stayed up there with Roy and I did a lot of thinking and Roy did a lot less drinking. He's a blacksmith and a talented one, at that. In the interim, I bought a 30-foot travel trailer. It's really nice and now I have a place up in northern Michigan to go to, near Roy's place. He's a good man and he's had a lot to do with my thoughts on alcohol, believe me, because he's got it bad but he's trying to get better. Really, that's all you can do is keep trying to get better. I told him if he gets down on his fucking knees he'll get better. You just have to pray your ass off. God will take care of you. As I write this, I've learned Roy has entered rehab and is on his way to sobriety. I'd like to think I played some small part in that.

I was getting ready to come back down state and my phone dings as soon as I come back into town. Roy's place doesn't get cell service so I was pretty disconnected while I was up there. I had a LinkedIn message from a girl that said, "I got Rottweiler from a Jerome Lill in 1981. Is this the same Jerome that I used to know who sold Rottweilers?" Her name was Karen Smith.

Now dig this, I have not talked to this girl since 1981. I never saw her or spoke to her after I sold her a dog — by the way, that dog became a grand champion Rottweiler and was on the cover of Dog World. Then after all that time — nearly 40 years — this woman contacted me. What's interesting is that the timing of this phone call confirms everything I ever said about God interweaving into our lives at very specific points in time.

Karen told me that she finished school and she got married to a guy who was a veterinarian. They had their own veterinary practice and had kids, and everything was going well. However, her husband got addicted to the narcotics that were readily available to him as a veterinarian. He was also a heavy drinker.

She became pregnant with their second child and when it was time for labor, she went to the hospital. She got a hold of her husband to pick up their three-year-old daughter from a sitter before coming to the hospital. He picked the girl up and, of course, he's under the influence of something and got into a car accident.

He doesn't get hurt but his daughter is paralyzed from the waist down. She will be in a wheelchair for the rest of her life.

Karen contacting me is not a coincidence. I don't believe that. I believe it's an act of Big Fats again. He needed me to tell her story because it's going to register with someone. Someone will be touched by her story and, perhaps, make changes in their life. God's watching your ass and He knows what you need to hear. You just have to listen to it.

Karen tried to deal with her husband's issues, but he's too sick. He ended up shooting himself because alcoholics only know how to feel sorry for themselves, not others. Suicide is a selfish act and instead of helping his two children and wife, he took the easy way out. Alcoholics don't think of other people. We say, "Oh I'm a good person, I care so much." Bullshit. You don't care about shit except your own selfish ass and remember that.

I left Michigan to head back to Sarasota to see Gregory. When I returned, I found out another friend of mine had to have the top of his liver cut off. I mean, he's got cirrhosis of the liver and he continued to drink. Everyone I knew who continued to drink after a serious health issue like cirrhosis ended up dead. Think about what it looks like to the person who finds you bleeding out from alcoholism. Think about it. Think about your epitaph. Is that a good one, really? I mean all these things that happen are just terrible when drugs and alcohol are involved.

Ben Rose, another friend of mine, knew someone who had problems with drugs and alcohol. He said the guy would quit and get better, start up again, quit and get better, start up again, over and over. He went to a drug dealer's house and got in a fucking argument over money. It's always something when it comes to money.

He got stabbed in the hip, but that didn't kill him. His hip became infected, he went septic, which traveled to his lungs and then he died. So whatever route you go with drugs or alcohol, you will die, you understand this? You may take somebody with you, too. Do you want to be responsible for that shit? How about Karen's husband who crippled his three-year-old? She's now doing really well and works in the entertainment industry but let's be honest; her father created a hurdle for her to have to jump over for the rest of her life. Do you want to leave somebody like that?

My buddy Roy up in Michigan has a pal who was drinking and drove to Roy's house.

Roy's daughter was getting married while I was up there, and here comes this guy up the driveway, beeping his horn. He's drunk on his ass.

So I sat him down and I said, "You idiot, what are you doing? You know you could kill somebody. You're going to kill yourself or you're going to go to jail but what the hell are you doing?"

Now, this guy is over 60 years old. That's pretty childish. He should know better after two DUIs already. He tells me he'll do better and he knows what I'm saying. A couple of weeks later, he's in the suburbs back down state and he gets another DUI.

Now he's in deep shit. Not to mention, he could have killed somebody. This is true for anyone who gets behind the wheel after they've been using or drinking. You could kill a baby, you could kill a family, you could kill a dog. You could possibly kill something or someone besides yourself and that's what you should think about.

You know what, if you're going to do something, *smoke some pot.*

It'll do you better and it's not going to rot your liver. You won't bleed out of your asshole from it and you won't get violent and hurt people.

I'm not telling you to become a pothead, be reasonable. I'm an advocate of marijuana and I think it benefits people in different ways from a medicinal standpoint. People should be more open-minded to it.

I'm going to continue to try to do good. Let's all go out and do good things. Pray, spread peace, pray some more, and Big Fats will help you. Don't fuck your life up.

Don't fuck anybody else's life up.

Don't kill anybody. Don't kill yourself.

Don't drive drunk. Go pray somewhere because it is all a God thing. I'm asking you to be a good person, don't fill yourself full of alcohol. That's about it.

Peace out and God bless you.

Tribute to a Friend

STEVE FARMER
December 31, 1948 - April 7, 2020

I needed to write this final story in honor and memory of Steve Farmer, musician extraordinaire, songwriter and guitarist with the Amboy Dukes.

One summer in the late 90s, I was living in Royal Oak, Michigan and spending a lot of time drinking and listening to music in a bar called the Bear's Den in nearby Berkley.

Just rockin' and rollin' — and drunk.

Now dig this; I worked for a lot of bands in the Detroit area as a roadie in the 60s. My friend Dick Sloss had got me a lot of different gigs with these bands. One of these bands was The Amboy Dukes, featuring Ted Nugent, then known as "The Nuge." The band had just released their hit single "Journey To The Center of the Mind." I'm sure Detroiters remember that.

Dick had told me the story of how Steve was a co-writer of the song, and had not received full credit for his contribution. Steve always felt frustrated that he had been denied the recognition due him.

So I go to the Bear's Den, and I find myself talking to this skinny, long-haired guy at the bar, wearing a headband, leather vest and no shirt, talking about old Detroit rock 'n' roll. I tell him the story Dick told me, mentioning Farmer's name. This guy takes out his wallet and his driver's license and slaps it on the bar. And guess who I'm telling this story to?

Steve Farmer.

I'm telling Steve Farmer his own fucking story!

To make a long story short, Steve and I palled around for a good while.

Steve was living in Redford, helping his mother and writing music, working on a new CD, "Journey To The Center of The Dark Side of Your Mind." Steve had a dark side when he was drinking, believe me.

One particular night, he was scheduled to play a gig at a theater in downtown Royal Oak. For some reason that gig got cancelled. Steve went ballistic at 2 a.m. in the morning in the middle of the street. We were both pretty drunk. Steve started swearing in the street at the top of his lungs, and spitting while throwing a stack of printed advertising flyers at the building!

As time passed, Steve hired me and Glen Heidrich to straighten his mother's garage in Redford.

During this period of time, Steve and I became close friends, and he confided to me that he was still hurt by the situation with The Dukes, and his co-author credit for their song.

Well Steve… here's your credit! Love ya miss ya brother.

Steve passed away in April of 2020. God Bless this very kind, intelligent and supremely talented Detroit musician. Your song still lives on in the hearts and minds of all Detroit rock and rollers, and anyone who loves great music my dear friend.

Carrying your equipment and being your close friend was, and still is, one of the finest, most memorable honors in my life.

Peace out my friend.

I'd say "God Bless You," but he already has.

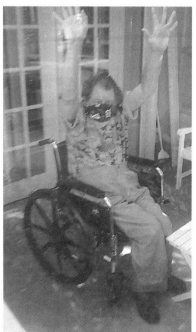

End of the book. Not the end of our lives! Gregory is alive and well in Sarasota. I'm alive and well in Detroit. Let's all be grateful we're all alive and well. There are those worse off than all of us...somewhere.

Peace out.